JOHARI'S WINDOW

Reviews

"I believe Suzy has achieved work of substance whereby the reader cannot fail to be moved and memories stirred. The book takes you on a lyrical journey which evokes the emotions. A feeling of deep love pervades throughout, whilst at the same time, a feeling of sadness for a loss that can never return… The descriptions colourful, sensuous and exotic, transporting the reader right into the author's memory. It is as if we are there with her in each vignette." – **Jennifer Carlton, Director of Carlton Academy, BA (Hons), Dip Couns. Dip Hyp/Master Practitioner N.L.P., P.G. Cert Ed.H.E.**

"This absorbing novel gives us glimpses of one life as it intersects with several others on a heightened emotional plane. This is a kaleidoscope of beauty. So much more than a romantic tale, *Johari's Window* offers glimpses without revealing, contains without restricting, understands its own deep story and shares it without simplification. Love has its own spectrum to examine on a journey of fluid lyricism. The heart is overflowing with fervour. The intelligence is deeply emotional. Somehow the tongue in this language is both visceral and mysterious. It is almost as though we are learning to use it for the first time." – **Katrina Plumb**

Johari's Window

SUZY DAVIES

Dear Vanessa. Thanks
for being in the world.
Love Suzy x

SilverWood

Published in 2014 by SilverWood Books

SilverWood Books Ltd
30 Queen Charlotte Street, Bristol, BS1 4HJ
www.silverwoodbooks.co.uk

ISBN 978-1-78132-283-3 (paperback)
ISBN 978-1-78132-284-0 (ebook)

British Library Cataloguing in Publication Data
A CIP catalogue record for this book is available from
the British Library

Set in Bembo by SilverWood Books
Printed on responsibly sourced paper

This book is dedicated to the memory of my late father, John, and my late mother, Joan. It is also dedicated to those who dare to feel.

Acknowledgements

I owe a debt of gratitude to many people who have faith in me and who have helped me in the genesis of this book.

Thanks, Edgar, for recording the audio version, which allowed me to hear the words, and to his long-suffering parents for use of the studio, and for tiptoeing round the house in the process.

Thanks too, to Linda for her technical computer support.

This memoir would not have been possible without the advice of my fellow writers: Ian Burton, Stephen Bingham, and Sharon Wright; and all those at Waterford Writers' Weekend in 2014 – thank you for keeping the creative spark alight!

Heartfelt thanks go to the very lovely Mrs Pontefract at Nuneaton's High School for Girls, and to Forward Poetry, who published my poems and encouraged me to write in the early days.

Sincere appreciation goes to Helen Hart and her team at SilverWood Books.

Thank yous go to Louise, Glenys, Debbie, Aggie, Beverley, Janice, Dorothy, Val, Julie, Alison, Pauline and Sue for old times and beautiful memories. Thanks to all my friends along the journey to where I am today – you know who you are! Special mentions go to my dear friends Nada, Anne, Kim, Anna and her daughter, Eva, Helen, Laura, Patricia and Jennie for all their moral support.

Finally, I wish to thank my family, and in particular my dear cousin, Vanessa, for guiding me through the darkness, for companionship, for giving me a sense of ontological security and the courage to carry on.

Prologue

I didn't imagine I'd come to writing like this. That it would be compulsive. That writing would be the oxygen my body depends on.

So what brought me here? I think I've been writing all my life, since I was a child. It started with singing, then oral storytelling, a tradition of the Welsh. Reading gave me a sense of otherness; it was romantic, exotic in its foreignness. I wanted to belong to that distant landscape.

Words are strange beings. There is a fluidity, a kind of openness about the spoken word whispered in the tympanum of your ear, in the dark. I can say that's not what I meant. Ask you to interpret the gesture of a gloved hand, my shadow-boxing, the face behind the mask. Ask you to conspire with me in my vague seduction. I want to become you, lose myself in you, if only for a moment. Let me make love to you through language.

Voyage with me a while, let me be recumbent. The sun's a fireball in the sky, a torch blazing above Death Valley. I luxuriate in the heat of your kiss. This is No Man's Land. You recline in the cool liquid shadows as the sun turns round. I thought I saw sunrise. Hush! Hush! No language! Hear the wind blow. It buffets the sand. The dunes heave.

I can see the caravanserai, like a mirage in the distance. The heat hums. I thought I saw water. What would you have on these trade winds for your comfort?

Winters are harsh, my lover. The snow-birds wing across the frozen tundra, black darts piercing the sky. Fading now, their mournful cries echo as the night unfolds a starry blanket.

Spring is when I see you amongst the blossoms, trees and lilacs.

Autumn's where you begin the dance, your ever-changing colours. The rain and the scudding clouds, a flash of blue; the ink still wet on the canvas.

The Colour of Sunlight
Streaming through a Water Bubble

It was one of those idyllic summers in Wales, in the great old mansion, Plas Antaron, where my grandmother lived for a peppercorn rent. The story went that the house used to be a nunnery. My mother, an empath, had visions of shadowy figures floating down corridors at dark and sailing through invisible doors. Some said that, once upon a time, it was a coaching house, where highwaymen, revellers, storytellers and travellers tethered their horses, drank ale, shared their troubles as easily as their fortunes, and bedded down for the night. For me, at the age of seven, it was my haven; a dreamy world in a liquid bubble. Love permeated the very fabric of the home. It was the kind of love that seemed to beckon you from a distance, drawing you in and sustaining you. This love remained in memories; in the infinite chambers of the heart.

Plas Antaron stood on a hill, nestling behind an island of trees in the centre of a semi-wild garden. A pair of wrought-iron gates, rusted at the hinges, were at the end of the drive, which led to a sturdy oak front door with a highly-polished brass letterbox and a grey slate front step. The hallway floor was mosaic: Victorian white and black.

Mrs Hughes lived downstairs. She remained in bed most mornings.

I remember that morning, standing there, in my own little dream world. In front of me was the sweep of a huge polished banister in oak, and a row of pegs for people's coats. They were empty, except for a single trilby with feathers in the band.

My mother's voice was fading into the kitchen. My father's voice echoed on the landing between English and our mother tongue. We were going to Pen Dinas.

"Come on, Cariad, you can't sit on the stairs now, can you!"

I hear voices in the distance, on the landing upstairs. My daddy's voice echoes on the landing – Boom! Boom! Boom! (He speaks half in Welsh and half in English like my grandma.) I want to run out ahead, under the arches that lead to the stables. It is cool there in the summer, and when I shout my voice is big. Sometimes, my friend shouts back.

I am sitting on the third step. Nearly time now. The lino gleams beneath the window of stained glass. I am thinking of Mummy and rainbow bubbles. My world is full of laughter, and stories of dragons and princesses and knights and castles and whales and frogs.

"There are wolves in the wildwood," Daddy says, "but they are kind, not bad."

(Susan was tracing imaginary patterns with her fingers as if she had a paintbrush. At her grandmother's words, she jumped up, pulled the elastic band from her hair, and raced perilously down the steps.)

I sit on the first step and tie my shoe, all by myself. Now I am standing at the giant doorway, and skip outside. Daddy won't be cross. I was good in the car and kept a look out for monkey caravans that have monkeys who are kidnappers, Mummy says, and the big sign with Croeso y Cymru.

The shadows on the baked tarmac are long. I dance, point my feet. We will be here for two weeks before ballet school, and days with Louise again. I am getting tall. There are bald patches, like Daddy's head, on the pebbledash, higher up than last year. I have picked off the stones. (I was a graffiti artist. No words, no pictures. The trace of identity marked in spaces.)

Still there is no one. The wait seems ages. A woodpecker is

drumming – tap, tap, tap – on the tree bark. "The jackdaws are comical!" (That's how my grandmother says it.) "They don't walk in a straight line like the other birds."

I was scared of the magpies. Once they stole my grandmother's hatpin, the one with the pearl. But they won't pick out your eyes.

Nearly time now…I race back, into the hallway. I climb the stairs to the kitchen where I am greeted with a chorus. "Where have you been?" they say in English and in Welsh. My father gathers me up.

Gwladys and Joan were getting a picnic ready. There was orange juice on the table. It was lukewarm. I poured Susan a glass. She was on a heavy chair at the old farmhouse table. Her legs just touched the leather-clad floor. Her grandmother had sewn together pieces of cow-hide. It was soft when her toes touched it. She was swinging her legs. That girl has so much unspent energy.

"You got ants in your pants!"

It will not be long now. They promised. And I have been good. But before we leave, grandma is going to feed the birds. "Come on, Bach," says my grandma, her bony hand reaching into the pantry, "you have to keep your hands flat, see, and then they won't hurt you!" Now we are alone. Mum and Dad have gone to load the car. "Quietly does it!" my grandma is saying, as she lifts the window.

The glass was very old and the cord a little frayed. Gwladys was gentle. Susan glanced at the pale, sensitive skin on her grandmother's conical white hands. The fingers were unusually thin and long. Her eyes were extraordinary. One was pale blue-grey like the sky, a long way from a storm. The other was more violet, with a splash of brown, like earth. She thought that a painter had flicked the colours into Granny's eyes when he had made her. Sometimes they looked like marbles. He had spun grey into the fading chestnut hair. Susan thought my mother-in-law was very lovely and graceful, and her neck was long. She was tall and, elegant like the actress and dancer Moira Shearer.

"Come, come. Come, come," she calls. Her voice is more sing-song than Mummy's. Her thin hand is now resting on the slate window ledge.

We waited and waited. Susie was wriggling. Sometimes there's no keeping her still, see. We heard a flutter. Then, there was a swoop and dive of wings. It was a small green bird. It landed in the palm of my hand, see. The little visitor feasted on the nut mix.

"Now it's your turn," Grandma says, her eyes looking into the distance.

More minutes waiting. But when the bird came, I pulled my hand away, imagining it would hurt. The seeds fell onto the shelf.

"If at first you don't succeed, try, try, and try again."

My mother used to stand at the gate, at Jules the Farm, calling the horses. They greeted her, nuzzling her face. They came to her even if she didn't feed them. She communicated with them in whispers, and they understood. And on children, too, she had a calming effect.

A Kind of Blue

There is rain; it is Monsoon season in Korea. Nothing is like rain for forgetting and remembering, for blurring names and faces, signs, into a myopic, watery picture. With the downpour come those memories of you, in soft focus.

"One two, one two." I have been walking for what seems like hours. My watch has stopped. Taxi, then. A streetcar pulls up. Standstill, and then the metal thud goodbye of a door as it closes. Stilettos launch out onto the tarmac. Someone has taken flight into the rain. As I watch her merge with the crowd, so too does her umbrella, glistening red-blue in a myriad of moving colour, mingling and combining to make one line. Moments later, the line decomposes, like the skin shed from a snake. The girl with the blue umbrella has slipped by into a blaze of light.

The streets are made of cast off ribbons now, as if Medusa herself were dancing there in the half-shadow and full neon that dazzles. Past the shops in Shoe Street and along Rodeo Drive, past the bars and the beautiful people, a solitary crowd is pressing on me. I look over my shoulder as I head for the park. Obama gazes down from a plasma screen in bright digital Technicolor.

I head off nearer to home where the silhouetted skyline of apartments sends me plummeting into a black and white negative. I am a floating thing. Rock, paper, scissors – I am Paper Bird. I exist.

As I inhale the memory of your colours in my darkness, I am suspended on a wire, delicate and strong, that cuts across the globe. I feel your voice cut across the wire. My heart slows with the rhythm, the rain beating against my window to the world. Outside are the mountains, strong as fortresses, high above the sea. And you carry me on the wire. And I float, a sleeping thing, a feather, down, down, down into a dream-saturated sleep.

Last night, I was dreaming of November. A firework burst of russet carnivalled the trees, and I dreamt of bonfires all over the little island. Someone lifted me high, high above the crowd, skywards. Someone was lifting me up into the velvet blackness of a star-spangled sky. There was the perfume of earth and rain and skin and gunpowder. He held me high, high up, until the last crash of gunpowder and the last limb melted with the fire. I sheltered my face in his shoulder, our backs together against the rain. And the whole of the earth turned to embrace us. And my heart fluttered like the wings of a bird in his hands.

The journey home was dark and silent. Rain was falling. Hypnotised by the swish of wipers – back and forth, back and forth – my eyelids closed. The smell of Embassy No. 1 invaded my nostrils. When we got home, it would be brighter than the Blackpool illuminations. And my father would gather me up – a sleeping thing, a rag doll – taking me across the threshold into the light. He would carry me up into the back room that looked out onto the quarry. But in the English summer, the distant view was masked by trees. And there'd be a golden haze of cornfields that reached forever into the sun.

Yellow

The landscape of the metropolis is lit with neon crosses: signs of faith, community and worship. From the rooftop, the cityscape shelters under a starless sky. A pale moon hangs over Palgong Mountain. And in the distance, lies the temple of the Sleeping Buddha.

A Canadian missionary is telling tales of barbarism and magic in South Africa. A young academic, separate from the rest of the group, rehearses his already fluent Spanish. And the psychologist sits and listens and observes, while his girlfriend, an artist, engages in a pyrotechnical display at the barbecue.

"A sign of mental derangement, to believe in a higher power you cannot see, or even talk to."

(Steak turned, paper cups, beer, lettuce, corkscrew, etc.)

"So what is the meaning of the Chinese lettering?" I had asked the guide yesterday.

"No meaning in itself. The colours specify the meaning of the words."

He proceeded from A to B; from red to white to blue.

"But I want to hear yellow," I say.

"Yellow? It signifies the earth; north, south, east, west; rebirth and creation...The centre of everything."

"Why don't you concentrate on what you're doing?" interjects the psychologist.

"But," replies the artist, "I am."

(I am sometimes torn between the two of them, a kind of go-between, so to speak.)

"We should have got out of the EU," re-joins the

psychologist. "We're going to get fucked unless the Irish…!"

The following afternoon, after a long night on the roof, I take off and find myself at Apsan Park. (There is much controversy about the origin of the trees.)

A shutter clicks. A child, smiling in the yellow glow that pours between the branches makes a V sign. A young family are gathered under a tree. It is cherry blossom viewing time. A gentle breeze is gathering the petals, lifting them up and up, trailing them this way and that – confetti on the wind.

"I am Rock Bird. Water-play, butterfly, cherry petals in her hair."

She lifts one cherry petal to her open mouth. She is sitting under a man-made waterfall on a stone tiled floor. Her dark, tranquil eyes watch the cherry petals float like little boats.

Last night, I was dreaming of Jeju-do. And as I made my descent, the trees and mountains were my compass. Where the two seas met, I found my special place. White sails rose into the sunlight, and grey rocks into curls of sea spray. In the distance, I had a bird's eye view of a winding trail around the backbone; where the Hallasan meets a bleaker sky. Yellow rolled round into the blue of the horizon. And I heard the Haenyo murmuring on the breeze. Their lives are a triumph over Nature's cruelties. They love, they sing, they dance. These women are warriors, wrestling with the waves. "How is it that the Haenyo have no fear of intimacy with the deep?"

A mermaid is singing, and she whistles as she is surfacing. I can hear her breathe. Now she offers me her catch. We surface together. And my lips are salt, and my hair seaweed. And it is you again; you are unravelling me. Only the stars are my north, my south, my west and my east. I offer you a shell. You hear my voice.

It is November. We are weaving through dense rush-hour traffic. An artist is withdrawing into her being, a kaleidoscope of stills moving before her eyes. As usual we are late, and as the taxi slows, I catch a glimpse of a small, close group flowing out of the building onto a floodlit terrace. In unison, they are clapping their hands. It is the opening night of *Madama Butterfly*.

The foyer is awash with lights. Heads turn to stare. I dip my head. Now they smile and bow to show their respect in return. The artist makes a sudden movement; she has caught her own reflection in the mirrored glass windows and in an instant, she is gone.

The group are studying the programme. Together, we are taking the elevator. Just as we find our seats on the balcony, the lighting goes down. In a cloud of Coco Chanel the artist emerges; a slow, secret smile on her new, fresh face.

An orchestra tunes up, the curtain lifts. A performance has begun. Hangul characters are on a screen before me. I am mesmerised by figures making their exits and entrances. They dance above the stage like gorgeous, ethereal clockwork dolls. Light kisses their chalk-white faces: blue-violet, red and indigo. I observe their command of space. Now they are close, and now a boatman carries the hero away and he is gone. My eyes can hear distant music, an almost unspeakable language. And I need you to explain. A butterfly in a gilded cage is amongst the glitter. A thousand cherry blossoms rain from the sky.

The evening closes. Clicks of flashlights capture fleeting smiles. The crowd disperses. Little groups go by, taking different directions. In the half-light, I can hear her voice as she begins retelling her story. I listen for diversions. It is distinct from my own.

Here is the bridge, and there the river, and at the memorial bell the artist is falling silent. She hugs me goodbye, her face soft with glimmers of dust-like powder. I watch as she retreats into the shadows, her satin dress shivering as she breathes in the night air.

Perhaps now, in the moonlight he'll be waiting at her

door. He's like that. And they'll kiss without words. And she'll tell him the story of her evening and her night amongst the stars. All night long they'll be making their story in their own special language. And in the morning, she'll look in the mirror as he makes the coffee and he'll cradle the cups with his bear-like hands. With sleepy nods he'll listen, and at intervals speak in monosyllables. And like Schehezerade she'll slip away, with some things left unspoken.

Enter left. The room is quiet. I have my books and my music. There is the faint scent of jasmine. And I am lying behind the rice screens, enveloped in the softness of the dark.

Among my possessions is a small book, and on the inside cover there are two names. I am searching for the word. Initials are inked on the spine, and at the turn of the page, the name, repeated again. I am holding a book in my hands and the memory of a thief claiming her lost territory.

I was an unwilling passenger leaving the Big Country. I would miss the mountains and waterfalls, the treks on broad horses' backs to hidden villages in secret valleys. I thought of boats, and fisherman at the docks with John Dory and mackerel, rainbows in their skins. And sharp-eyed cockle women, when the tide turns, making a living. And the bird-woman, special to me, with paint-splashed eyes. She had a faraway gaze like my father's.

As the car sped on its journey, I thought of Jules the Farm and Jones the Lodge and Sharon with tousled hair, and one sock up and one sock down from Penparcau. I missed her already. I was leaving the high road with armfuls of wild flowers, and the low road with the strange toll house that led from Devil's Bridge to the old house with iron gates and the grey Welsh slate that we called Plas Antaron.

As the car continued on its way, in my mind's eye I was climbing high – high up Pen Dinas Head amongst sparkling yellow gorse, sea birds and white heather, with the oily sheep huddled together against the wind. High, high up, the wind moulded the treeless landscape and stunted bushes so the sea and the big sky were one and people small. I was lost in the sound of the sea of a thousand summers. The car was full of talk. And silently, as the pages unfurled, I was looking for the words of 'Swallow of the Mountain', but there were none. As the lights twinkled in the northern hemisphere, I whispered to myself, "*Nos da*, but not forever."

The Colours He Is

Just a painting, but it evokes memories. In the morning light, a shadow falls on Mrs Clark and Mr Clark basks in the sunshine, sensuous as the lap cat I know a certain Morley would despise. The painting is by David Hockney. Mina and I were in the Tate when I bought the reproduction.

"Where have you got to?" came the voice. "I've been here half an hour!"

The Mina Khan that I used to know – carefree, happy-go-lucky, prepared to leave destiny to the capricious hand of chance – had now taken on the mantle of the legal profession and had made it her own.

The suffocation on the tube, the clinging crowd and the polluted heat were beginning to grate. I was thankful that I could just step inside. She'd be there as she was in the old days. I was just opposite Chez Gerrard where the ambience, if a little lacking in sophistication, was light and convivial. It was the sort of establishment frequented by itinerants and young executives who were something in the city. We could say whatever we wanted.

As I climbed the steel staircase that led to the restaurant, I cast my eyes around for Mina, but she was nowhere. Maybe, in a flurry of impatience, she had gone into the cobbled streets with mime artists, tarot readers and jugglers, into the sunshine.

Was it, or wasn't it her? Alas, there had been many missed meetings, so many last-minute apologies. Maybe I'd erased the memory of her face. Maybe, maybe it's you? I moved a little closer, but didn't repel her as a stranger would; a slow look of recognition dawned.

I knew it was her, tottering inelegantly on her Choos, and a little worse for wear. Gone was the sleek, glossy bob cut I had so admired, and hello now to a mass of big retro-style hair, which almost perceptibly extended. It was actually 'M'.

Meeting once more, memories came flooding back. When first I met Mina, she was at the bus stop. A gluey mass stuck on the curb stone which looked like gum. I shot her a glance and she hunched her shoulders. It was not her. The bus was crowded, so I sidled in beside her. Together we rode. On arrival at Highmeadows, the red-light district, a stone's throw from college, it seemed appropriate to offer her coffee at my flat. We talked until morning, and the chirping of birds.

I remember now, M, Byron and me at Regent's Park, and a performance of *La Bohème*. Byron pursued me, and women like to bite and scratch. Then law school, and phone calls from York. Mina detested her lodgings; they were dampening her spirits, so cold were the winters there. And later, there was the story of Mina and Astrid, her lipstick lesbian romance. She had returned to the Midlands, and now Mina was teaching art, a better occupation than lugging carcasses at a meat factory. When first she moved to London, M loved to be seen with the movers and shakers in West End nightclubs. One evening she pawned a watch to get a taxi home. And finally, she took up lodgings in Bethnal Green. There she settled for a limp recruitment consultant, which I knew wouldn't last.

These days I remember her as she used to be: M and her infatuations; M always forthright, insensitive, untidy, reliable, passionate, caring, trustworthy, and loyal. She had a mastery of language so rarely seen in native speakers who are gifted from birth. She chose her words as she chose her perfume. Did they reflect the mood, the occasion? She seized the moment – how I've thanked her privately for that.

"You're living on borrowed time," she stated. The economy of words, and something in the way her body subtly shifted towards me as she pinned me to the wall with her eyes, told me the required response. I imagined her in court. There was such power in those small hands. She had given me permission to renege on my duties, to get him out once and for all.

"And whatever happened to the nice guy," she said, in a discreet tone. "The one you, er, felt something for?" She seemed to be scrutinising the brush strokes; her shoulders shielding me from a matronly guide with flat, practical brogues, and a gushing group of luvvies who clutched glossy art catalogues and London guides: ladies who lunched and had not lost all hope. Everything was 'darling'. M knew about the love with no name, the one for which we draw breath and then stand back.

"Morley was, is, beautiful like that painting," I said.

"So, why do you love him?"

My emotions flew to the painting and back, yet he was somehow more than that.

"I just like the colours he wears, the colours he is," I answered evasively.

Rhythm

Barcelona. And where are you, my lover? Everywhere I see your face. Wherever I am in the world I cannot forget you. Dance with me; I am a fighter, but my fight is not with you. I want to dance with you into the sunset; I want to kiss you at sunrise. I want to know you, for you have touched the gypsy in my soul. Quietly, you have always been behind me, watching, waiting for my soul to be reborn. I loved you, but your quiet power came between us. But now, I have grown. Why not stand up and say it?

The streets are a collage of my emotions. I want to write you, I want to sing you. Something in you, I cannot capture. And the gypsy's feet keep dancing to the flamenco of her soul.

"You know," said Avril at my grandmother's funeral, "that we are descended from the gypsies." She was my father's cousin, blessed and cursed for her beauty, a TV producer, but no one would believe she could be beautiful and intelligent. I listened to what she had to say. And I know I am not English, so I read these streets from in-between somehow.

Show me a people who are oppressed, and I'll show you passion and poetry and singing from the valleys. I come from a place where there is no shame in saying "I love you" as loud as a bell, or shame in striking the heart with the beat of a drum.

Tonight, the opera was magical. Beneath the glistening crystal giddy couples were holding hands. Then, an audible gasp and hush from the crowd as an usher guided us into the auditorium. The Spaniard stroked my hand as we awaited our turn.

I remember singers and dancers pouring out onto the

boards, under dimmed spotlights. They were dressed in white and red and black. The Spanish blues or *letres* spoke of boat-people, of fishermen and danger, and of loss and anger. They spoke of betrayal. And sometimes they spoke of love. And love was waiting for an answer.

Slowly, slowly, I relax, lulled by the dulcet cante of the prima donna's voice. And then andante, andante, the male principal returns a warm, flowing bass, and she dances. His steps marry hers in rhythmical staccato, grounding me, lifting me high and low, and grounding me. "Listen!" they say in unison. The steps are alternating, as the gypsy boy drums his feet defiantly. It is clear they are quarrelling. Now the lady resists his advances. And now, her shoulders say she's following. His proud erect head turns away. Later, his torso seems to mirror the smooth curve of her naked back. There is something in the way his night moves play her into a line of attack.

"Flamenco, my flamingo."

(But this is love.)

"Something." (Audible)

"Are you okay?" (In Spanish)

My dress, black. And the voice is returning in a soft blue light, which gives an answer to her voice just as the steps marry the guitar. Coming. Hear.

(They say: He kisses away the pearls of sweat in the small of her back.)

Some time passes.

Two people exit, stage left.

In the foreground, there is a tent. There is a background of the sea and the mountains. And all above us, the bright canopy of stars. Clothes and flower petals are strewn on the bare earth. Amongst them is a pair of red shoes, and a black fedora hat.

Camera pans the audience – no one is there. A pair of opera glasses remain on a chair.

The Colour of a Rose

Picture the scene, wartime Britain. A blonde Amazonian woman is gazing down from an upstairs window of a Dundee hotel. Into the frame appears a group of sailors. One of them is striking, with golden, copper-coloured hair. My mother, playing the tomboy, whistles, and as he looks up, something cascades from the window: a red rose. That's how they met.

They held a wordless conversation. And she blew him a slow, soft kiss. Perhaps it was something in the way he smiled or maybe her brazenness. She didn't know, but he hoped to see her again and found out her name and address.

He wrote to her from Gibraltar. At the end of the letter he wrote, 'Breakfast at Tiffany's'. I think he meant love, whatever that was. And they always spoke in their own special code.

I've rarely heard the song, except on the Silver Screen, but in Spain, from behind a billowing white curtain in an upstairs tenement, down, down the song floated. And my heart rippled, skipped a beat, because I think I know now, what it meant.

Blue: Midnight in Winter

My earliest memory of my mother is at a sewing machine. Piles of material: chiffon, lace and taffeta and ribbon adorned the dining room table. "What colour is best?" she asked me. So I answered. And with the skill of a draughtswoman, she cut the pieces, patternless. And she showed me how to pink the edges into a kind of zig-zag. Scissor-Bird. The circles from wrist to shoulder got bigger, giving the effect of a bluebell flower. She pinned each piece without any tacking, and into the hall she went. She was holding up the jigsaw, looking into the mirror. The dress was like these lines, put together out of remnants and fragments. The colour suited her – blue: midnight in winter. Her beauty, her allure, was transient as the snow.

That afternoon we fought about the bathroom, and she went in first. So defiantly I ironed my hair. (A kind of burning smell took over the house.) I struggled alone, putting on my first pair of stockings to go with the pale blue dress. Dad waited downstairs; his eye was on the clock. He was awkward in a black dinner jacket and tuxedo, leaving the bow tie till last. His shoes were mirrors. I could see my face in them.

"Is she ready yet?" Dad said, leaning forward in his favourite chair, his eyes bright with excitement.

"I'll look," I said.

Down the stairs swept the dress. Someone who resembled my mother, her hair piled up in a French chignon, her eyes grey, like blue steel. She looked luminous, magnificent in her remoteness.

At the annual ball, I clung to my father as he launched

me into the officers' mess. And all heads turned to see my mother, but my father turned to me and said, "You can have a glass of champagne but go easy!" The room was round with wood panelling, and there I was, talking to strangers, happily oblivious to age or rank or forms of address. I knew that when in doubt you kept silent. And the soldiers topped up my glass until my father said, "That's enough, she's only eleven."

"Is she?" they said in unison.

When it came to the time to dance, it was me and the Captain's daughter. And then, every man in the room was in my mother's orbit. But my father, a man's man, chatted with his friends and if he was jealous he concealed it well.

So finally, at the end of the evening, my parents took to the floor. A rugby player in his youth, my dad was stocky, but light on his feet and quick, and the chignon in my mother's hair began to fall. She was like a dream, and so like Grace Kelly, everyone whispered. But my father's eyes were warm and watchful and he was as magnetic as his gaze. There was one more dance that seemed to last for ages. Over my mother's shoulder, he was holding me in his gaze. His eyes were bright as a beacon; a sign to get the coats, as soon we would be going.

Home. How my father loved it. Back to the order of a house all ship-shape and everything in control. And with a shrug of the shoulders, off came the coat and the dinner jacket and the bowtie as soon as he entered the door. (He hated formalities, or stuffiness, but he followed protocol to the letter.) We changed back into casual clothes.

Then my mum and I could dance to the 45s we liked: 'The Preacher Man', 'Itchycoo Park', 'Waterloo Sunset' and 'Those Were the Days'. (Mary Hopkins was Mrs Hughes' niece.) My father, a cigarette burning out in his nicotine-stained fingers, said, "Put Sinatra on."

From the gramophone came the scratchy drawl of a voice talk-singing, "Witchcraft".

It was past the time to go to bed. Sleepy-eyed, I whispered goodnight to Marc Bolan – there was a picture of him above my pillows. Sometimes, in a darker mood, my father commented, "What he needs is a few years in the army and a good haircut. That'd sort him out!" It became his battle cry as he took down the poster. But I was strong willed, and as soon as the storm abated, the poster would appear again. And my father would pay him civil inattention, and I could sing and dance with Marc Bolan and say goodnight to him, and my father wouldn't breathe a word.

Purple, all the things unsaid,
A sunlit blackbird's feather
Tiger Lily
The burn of rubber. The sky. Heated
amethysts. The darkness.
Sometimes, your tongue, dancing.
Rothko. In moments of madness.
The possibility of writing something…

One of the women's children is wearing a pair of ballet shoes. She likes to dance. And I think of Nottingham and the ballet school, and Louise, my first ever friend.

We are sitting high, high on a bench, and I am staring at our satin feet. Pink ribbons, criss-crossing at our ankles. They are swinging in unison. We are waiting for lessons in dancing.

It's a long way up to the ceiling, and a big jump down to the floor. A woman with small feet, they say, can run away easily.

I watch my friend's little girl (also Louise). See her skip, and hop, and jump. What does she know about Mummy running? I wish she didn't have to know. Sometimes I hear her in the middle of the night. Wide awake. The tap, tap, tap of her feet on the ceiling. Then nothing. Asleep.

My pillow is slightly damp: trouble with my contact lenses, the dust, or something.

"Everything will be alright when the tiger lilies are out," Angela had said, and feet are good for flying.

I was twenty-five when I got my wings. People thought we were angels in the sky. There to seduce with soft words, and to serve food and drinks. Some of the romance is true. But with their heads in the clouds people can get lost in illusions. Most of all, we were chosen to save lives, and hide the fact behind manicured nails and painted-on smiles.

So when there was a suspect package on the plane the passengers learnt something I didn't fully know myself. We stayed on, until the last passenger was safely off. And if it was my time to go, then so be it; my Maker knew. It wasn't fatalism, it was duty.

Colin, when we promised to marry, said that flying wouldn't do. Yet he liked to mention it in passing: "My wife used to be an air stewardess, you know."

I think I was an executive wife, although I didn't know. Michael was my boss. A married man with kids, he was atypical for a man in a suit, and not at all staid. I couldn't park. He paid my parking fines. And when the sales figures were good he said, "Sue, we're really flying!"

We used to race up and down the motorway, and Jason, the boy-racer in the office, was a legend in his own lunch hour. Grantham to Peterborough in twenty-five minutes in an Alfa Romeo – oh yeah! (Dad and I, when I was young, used to go to Silverstone. To this day, I can't help liking the smell of burnt rubber and petrol.)

The village where Colin and I used to live wasn't in the wilds, it was commuter belt. How I laughed when some of the townies appeared on weekends, dressed in cloth caps and moleskins with the regulation wellies, just for a walk round the garden. But John, a young farmer, hid the family silver and the family tree from all but his friends. If he looked like a tramp, and his face was weathered, and his hands were chaffed with the wind, it was because he cared for the flock and worked the land.

Angela (another neighbour) and I became friends. About twelve years my senior, she was a countrywoman and a superb cook. She persuaded me to bake cakes for charity events in the village. With her I couldn't refuse; she had a way of asking in a charming Worcestershire burr with, "Will You?" and "Thanks!" before you'd even said yes. I couldn't cook fish. She told me to get a fish kettle. I never did. We used to do a circular walk together of about six miles on a Sunday, and then she'd make a cup of tea and always in bone china. She came to my house at Christmas for sherry and homemade mince pies. I loved her as if she were a sister.

The trouble was she started to drink. She didn't like getting hit, and it hurt a lot more if you were sober. The police in that county were good. He had to leave the house for two years, they said. When the spring was approaching, one day in her garden Angela turned to me and said, "Everything will be alright when the tiger lilies are out."

She looked at the empty bed wistfully. They came. They went. My marriage was over. But we were friends.

"As amicably as possible," we said.

That autumn I left. I tried to keep in touch. A letter came, written in green ink in a sprawling hand. It was from Laurence, the retired theology teacher. He collected scrap cars and stored the parts in his overgrown garden.

Gerald was a freemason. He wouldn't come in. He had to go. I never saw her again: suicide, sleeping pills and the bottle.

An Encounter

Goodbye Vienna. The hostel is more spartan than I thought, a gap in the curtain letting the light through. Leonard Cohen wrote about that somewhere in a song.

Tonight will be a first. I'm going to a restaurant alone. I head for the Irish Quarter.

"No thanks, I don't want to taste it!"

The waiter pours a glass of crisp white, and I settle for the salad. I've bought a book of Czech grammar. I have six weeks to learn enough Czech to survive. I light a cigarette. Smoke signals, and the comforting illusion that my late dad is somewhere not far off.

The restaurant is small. It's the kind where undiscovered couples go to share close secrets that only the darkness would know.

The baritone spoke. "Why don't you join me?"

He had nice eyes, but light, not dark. He had a steady gaze. But he was clearly a businessman in a suit. I hesitated.

"I'm okay, really!" I said.

"Oh, just join me, for a glass!" he said.

"No, really," I said, "but thank you."

But with a smile, he insisted. He moved my glass to his table. His confidence made me laugh. And so, I relented.

"I'm Johannes."

I liked his hands. They were warm and firm.

"I'm Sue."

"Do you live in Prague?"

"No, I'm on vacation. You?"

"Business," he said. "I'm a doctor."

(Trust me?)

He was handsome enough. But the eyes didn't have it.

"Where do you live?"

"Berlin."

We talked about the Wall. Did I speak German?

"A little."

The wine flowed into dessert. I judged he was a good lover from the way he shared his food, lingering over it. A layer of mayonnaise coated his sensuous mouth.

"I got divorced a few years ago," he volunteered. "My ex-wife visits my sons, but you know, it's lonely."

Over the years a tinge of cynicism has crept in.

"Yes, it can be."

"I'd like you to come to Berlin and meet my sons."

(He wiped his mouth with a white linen napkin, and monitored my response. Sons: a complication, perhaps. What do I know about being a mother?)

"How long are you going to stay?"

(How long have I got? My glass was empty; I paused, tapping my finger round the smooth, tinkling rim of crystal.)

"Not long, I'm doing a teaching course."

"At least let me see you safely to the door," he said persuasively. "My hotel is only at the end of the road. We could take a taxi together."

"Okay," I said.

The taxi driver was silent, which let us talk. The hotel came up first, the kind with revolving doors. Some footmen dressed in red and gold and white and black approached the taxi for luggage, but there wasn't any.

"Please stay with me tonight. A beautiful woman like you shouldn't be alone," he whispered, his hand fleetingly stroking the velvet of my shoulder.

"No, not really," I replied, shrinking away.

"Then promise me you'll come to Berlin, and give me your number." He handed me a business card; the texture suggested quality. It seems he was, after all, a doctor.

"Maybe I'll be able to," I replied. I felt the involuntary sting of tears, the emptiness of solitude. His lips pressed closer, against my cheek.

On his departure, he glanced swiftly back as he passed the furtive gaze of the gloved footmen. He was swept away in the momentum of shimmering glass. I thought he was pleasant. But I had seen how the world turned. And I was beginning to feel my own power.

Bohemia

11pm. It is the last tram. Sebastian and I have had a long day. I am watching the scenery fly by. There are factories; ugly, majestic and cumbersome, relics from some bygone era, before the Velvet Revolution. Tower blocks of stark concrete, and the never-ending intrusion of advertising hoardings: a bleak urban landscape.

In the distance, I can see the hills of Moravia and the winding river. I can see the faces of the children and factory workers. I can hear Smetana and the words of a poet.

The tram rumbles along the line and Sebastian and I are silently comfortable together, tired from teaching practice. His shoulder begins to sleep and touches mine. And then my head sinks down onto his shoulder. Minutes pass.

With a jolt, we awake. It's the end of the line. How to get back? We'll walk beside the line. It was the last tram. Minutes pass. He put his hand in mine, and our mouths touched.

At the hotel, all was quiet and dark. We crept in. Sebastian criss-crossed the corridor, and whispered, "Goodnight." Minutes passed. And I could hear Smetana and the lines of the poet, and I yearned for the place I belonged. And it left me wondering, the key cold in the lock.

"M," I said, "I've met someone!"

"Yeah, what, on the course?"

"Mm, blonde hair, blue eyes. Reminds me of Colin, only really sociable. There's a bit of an age gap. He's only twenty-seven, but looks older."

"Are you sure it isn't on the rebound?"

"From who, Colin?"

"Yeah."

"No, that was over in 1990."

"So what are you going to do? He's not moving in with you is he?"

"No, maybe we'll keep in touch, weekends, cos it's long distance."

"Do you ever see Morley?"

"No."

"Do you ever think about him?"

"I'd rather not talk about it."

"Oh."

"Anyway, why don't you stay with Byron? He could meet you at Heathrow."

"But I thought you...?"

"No. Met someone. I'll introduce you. He's got a family like the Waltons. But you and Byron!"

"I don't fancy him. He's not my type."

"But he's very fond of you. He likes you a lot. Anyway, he'll pick you up at the airport."

"Separate bedrooms."

"Separate bedrooms?"

"He's got a spare room."

"He won't try!"

"So, what's in it for him?" A hint of cynicism came creeping in.

"I told you!"

"What?"

"He finds you attractive, and he likes you a lot."

"That worries me. I don't want to give him the wrong impression!"

"You won't!"

"Tell him I'm still not over our separation. And I'm not divorced."

"Okay."

"Separate bedrooms."

"Separate bedrooms."

The line goes dead. Voices tail off.

"Hi, it's me!"

"Sue, how's it going?"

"Okay, busy though."

"Yeah, is it going okay?"

"Mm, we finish Thursday."

"Good – Byron really wants to see you. Says you can stay for a long weekend if you want. He's made up the spare bed!"

"Already?"

"Yeah. He's so looking forward to…"

"There won't be any problem."

"Absolutely not!"

"Okay. I may stay till Monday, then!"

"Good. We'll have more time."

"Only thing is, Art's back from Hong Kong, and I've got to cook dinner. The fridge is empty!"

"Who's Art?"

"Er…didn't I tell you? My flat share!"

"So you've moved someone in. You're a dark horse! What about the Italian?"

"It all ended with a chicken in a taxi!"

"What the fuck!"

"Tell you later."

"So who's this Art? Sounds complicated!"

"Well, it isn't. It's platonic."

"He's got a girlfriend? Or is he gay, or what?"

"He's not gay. I don't know if he's got a girlfriend. He's away a lot."

"It sounds complicated to me!"

"Well, it's not!"

"But you're cooking him dinner?"

38

"Yeah. He'll be tired. But there's nothing in it! Nothing. It's an arrangement!"

"Can't he cook then?"

"Yeah, but you know, fry-ups."

"So you *are* coming?"

"Yeah, we land Friday at ten."

"Byron said he'd wait for you."

"That's so nice of him!"

"He wants to know what you want for dinner. He's cooking, not a take out."

"Anything. Chicken? Maybe salad?"

"Okay."

"Mark and I will see you Saturday. I'm going to cook!"

"You cook?"

"Yeah."

"Chilli con carne, then!"

"How did you guess?"

Laughter.

"Is it dodgy where you live?"

"Late at night, it is. But Byron will bring you."

"What use would he be in a fight?"

"Well, you'll be taking a taxi."

"Yes, it will be like old times. I've really missed you."

"Me too!"

"And I can't wait to meet Mark."

"I think you'll get on. I'm going to have lots of children!"

"Listen, I'll see you soon!"

"Cool. See you Saturday!"

"Can't wait. Bye!"

"Bye."

Sometime in late summer, a launderette in High Meadows – I can't remember exactly. The washing is turning round. I want to get it over and done with. Enter Art.

He was tall, dark and handsome; in fact, drop dead gorgeous. Young though. What's he doing, examining the machines? And doing washing dressed in a suit? I bury my head in a magazine, pretend to read. He clears his throat.

"Is this always open on Sundays?"

"Yes."

"Is it always empty like this?" His eyes are dazzling water-pools of blue.

"Not always, but better than in the evenings."

Sitting in launderettes makes me sleepy; the repetitive drone of the machines, the clammy warmth. Did I want to go for a walk in the park, he asked. It was a waste of a nice day to be stuck indoors. He was dressed in a suit because he'd come from church. There would be plenty of people in the park. And so, I accepted.

We talked about his family up north. He was an engineer; MA from Sheffield. He had a sister who was divorced. His parents were happy. They had stayed together through the years. He liked his job, but he wanted to invent something. As he talked, I felt the sort of warmth that you might feel for a brother. He was very good-looking, but my pulse wasn't racing. I liked him, that was all.

Meeting on Sundays became a kind of habit. All we did was talk. One day, I confided my financial worries.

"I'm going to get a flatmate," I said.

All my friends were fixed up. His eyes met mine. He seemed to be thinking, but he kept quite silent.

Sundays with Art. Sometimes we took a walk along London Road to the Botanical Gardens.

"Are you still looking for a flatmate?" he said.

"Yeah."

"Do you mind if it's a guy?"

"No. Not at all! It would help with changing light bulbs."

He laughed.

"Well, you've done all right so far!" he said, shifting from foot to foot.

"Yeah, but the ceilings are high, and I have to borrow a ladder."

We walked along a little, by the small pond with the water lilies and the carp.

Art announced, "I've thought of someone."

"Oh, is he a friend?"

"I think you'd get on great."

"Who is it?"

He didn't reply; he was deep in thought, and so I added: "How well do you know him?"

"Really well!"

His face took on a seriousness I hadn't seen before.

"I've known him all my life!"

"Who is it?" I asked again.

"Is it okay if he comes to your place next Sunday?" he asked, looking at me side-on.

"Will you come too?"

"Yes, I promise I'll be there!"

He burst into a kind of creased-up laughter.

"What's funny?"

More laughter.

"The guy is me!" he said.

"I'd really like to share with you," I said shyly, "just as friends."

"Sure," he agreed.

We stood together, staring into the distance. The sky was a mirror to the earth, onto which mackerel clouds were fast encroaching, the foreboding steel grey fabric swallowing the last drops of light that were trying to squeeze through. It looked like rain.

We parted ways. And as I climbed the sweeping stairs

that led to my top floor flat, I remembered. It was as if I was viewing it for the first time. The agent could hardly believe the brisk tour. But it felt right; I loved the approach. The staircase itself was breath-taking: it belonged to an old movie, perfectly suitable territory for captivating a heart with the swish of a silk dress descending. I must confess the shadowy daydream contained a whisper of you.

I remembered, when I viewed, the narrowness of the hall. It needed a mirror. The pictures from the bedroom, *Mr and Mrs Clark and Percy* and *A Bigger Splash*, could go there. *Sergeant Pepper's Lonely Hearts Club Band* went back into my room, near the chimney breast. I put some photos on the wall. The lounge, which Art would sleep in, was light and airy. There was a pink chaise longue as a centrepiece, maybe not to Art's taste, and an inglenook for a desk. A wide TV screen was in one corner, and a collection of pirated black and white movies stacked on the floor. There were maybe about thirty, *Casablanca, Gilda* and *Sunset Boulevard* amongst them. The decor was neutral, with billowing cream curtains that touched the floor. In winter it would be warm and comfortable.

I found a new place for my wardrobe – the bathroom; the biggest bathroom I had ever known. In Victorian times it was a bedroom. Below it was the green of the garden. Here, by the window, it needed a chair. It could be a dressing room as well. No lock. Would I mind if he saw me in the raw? I decided that if I glimpsed him by accident, it would be like viewing a handsome work of art. You looked from a distance, and touching was off-limits. He'd feel the same, I thought.

The kitchen, then? Not enough work surfaces. It had a good colour scheme: red, white and blue with a second-hand café table, just big enough. 'The Cupboard' was too small to be a snug. My desk could go in there. Why hadn't I thought of that before? I bought some vanilla scented candles. And white fresh flowers. That night, I slept well.

In a flight of fancy one day, I had crossed the park. How lovely it would be to live there, I thought, on a summer's day. In my imagination, living there would be as close to living by the sea as you could get in the city. The changing spectacle of people playing ball, the fair and the funfair rides, the time of the carnival, the drift of music playing in the park, and couples, lost in conversation, walking hand in hand – people-watching. I had to take it; I needed time to breathe, time to write. The wind was blowing across the great expanse. Up above the street, I was walking the mountains. I was flying.

That first autumn, from the wide windows that let in the light, I saw an Arab woman, her yashmak like an ink-black sail, almost taking off, and the pigeons swirling about her head. Seagulls, paper kites; she was feeding them bread. She looked like a shaman dancing in a trance-like state.

I want to send you a note – I forget the words – written in the sand; a telepathic message that you will catch on the breeze across the waves:

BE MY CASTAWAY – PAPER BIRD

In the winter, we can fly away, or build a nest, waking to listen to the soft silence of the first snowfall.

The Colour of Sound

I remember an evening in winter. By the pond with the water-lilies, and the archway with climbing plants, brittle twigs now, in the frost.

Shameem and I fumbled through the dark together, crawled through the gap in the hedge, and scrambled down the slope into the Botanical Gardens, invisible as ghosts. I'd taken the Italian there. It had taken some persuasion.

"There's nothing to see," he said. He let go of my hand, and put his hands in his pockets. He was standing opposite me now, and his eyes darted from side to side, his feet indicating the way home. The city of Antonio's favourite Elmore Leonard books and noir movies was his thing. He disliked the wilderness; it was empty without people.

That night Shameem and I slipped out, into the darkness. I was walking, trying to forget you, as if each step could take me further and further away from how I was feeling. The fog was a blanket, muffling all sound, as snow does. A lamp glimmered through the glass window of the groundsman's cottage. On a low wall was the faint shimmer of a silvery trail, and a broken shell, cracked by a bird. Shameem and I stood there, huddled together, breathing our thoughts, where only the night heard. The vapour of our breath encircled the luminous green-blue notes which were hanging there.

The piper never knew we were watchers. Smoky blues of plaid were just visible against the dark green of the waxy foliage. Sounds echoed – sounds of a Scottish love song. They echoed through the silence, soft and melancholy, as he kept time on the earth with his foot, and the metal of the bagpipes glinted through faint moonshine, and lifting fog.

Home

I am coming in to land. I've done this trip many times, so no fear of flying. Heathrow is busy, and we hover above the Thames. I wonder how Byron has spent the night. Problems at Vienna: a missed plane. Poor Byron, it is just like him to wait.

Prague was beautiful in the rain, brushed in watercolour, bringing back blurry pictures in which my hapless father stood with his weathered, jovial face. Sebastian and I both cried as we said our farewells. We revisited the clock and the square and Charles Bridge, and I wondered how many others had stolen kisses in the spring, above the river, the big sky stretching before them. It looked different on a sunless day.

I wondered about my people: Eastern European gypsies that Avril had spoken of as the earth thudded softly on the coffin. She was a storyteller, I knew that much.

I thought of the school with the Russian head, and teachers, mainly Czechs and Poles. The aesthetics teacher, a man with a mobile, sensitive face, invited me to join the staff, and offered me his flat. He was a keen photographer. Natural light cut through the skylights, and at night you could survey the stars. But Sebastian said, through gritted teeth and a choked voice,

"He wants you for himself and we're going back."

At the rail station in Prague he stroked my head, cradling it and the sides of my face in his rain-soaked palms. His hungry tongue explored my throat.

"Keep it!" he said.

I wore his jacket. And in Prague, we parted.

*

I am coming in to land. And there will be Byron and Mina and her M. Art will be back to Reddington on Monday. I feel glad. There are so many happy memories; the have and have not of you. Obsession: a crazy dream, halfway between love and madness. I miss the thrill of you, my fix, and the impossible possibility of running in slow motion to you. I am obsessed, a thing enraptured.

"Is love about possession?" one of my students asks.

"There are different kinds of love," I hear myself say.

I answer as honestly as I can. And with some control I add, "Love is about understanding and reciprocity, but sometimes is a dangerous kind of knowing."

The scientist is making notes. His skills are advanced. Love is a serious business of exchange in Korea – you have to succeed. I ask some questions. It seems they comprehend.

Today one of my students told me I'm logical. He wishes he could think like that. "I had a good teacher," I said, with a flourish.

Heathrow was a breeze. It was familiar territory. I collected the suitcase (I always travel light), and Byron was there to meet me. We shook hands, and half embraced.

"It's so good of you, waiting like this," I said. "I had trouble at Vienna."

(Sometimes a lingering goodbye softens the blow.)

"You must be tired," he said.

"A little."

"Do you feel like dinner?"

"I don't mind, what about you?"

"I've cooked some coq au vin," he continued, "and I've brought your favourite wine from the cellar."

"That's great," I said. "I'm beginning to get an appetite."

He switched on the radio. Heart, I thought – good station. We were on our way to Wood Green, to the terraced house where M and I had turned up unannounced and hurled stones at an upstairs window. In those days, she had more front than Harrods.

When we got to the house, it was mid-afternoon. My mobile was off; I didn't check the calls.

"Take a pew!" he said, offering me the sofa. "I don't know about you, but I fancy a drink. Or would you like a coffee?"

"A drink would be perfect!"

"Why don't you come downstairs – I'll show you my wine collection."

"Maybe later, if you don't mind."

He shuffled to the cabinet, and took out two pristine cut-glass wine glasses. "Fleurie," he said, "the bouquet reminds me of you." I blushed. With some careful negotiation, this was a local difficulty any diplomat could get through.

The visit to Mina's went without a hitch. We stood in the long narrow kitchen with a view of back to back, washing up. She didn't want to sleep with him, a barrister, to secure her first appointment. Would I give her a reference? She planned to have a summer wedding, and go to live in Kent.

The men engaged in banter in the lounge. They were fans of Margaret Thatcher; we didn't join them. At about 9.45, we all ventured out. On the way to the pub, we talked about the Krays. We were on their old stomping ground. Someone launched a beer bottle over a high wall. It missed Mina's face by inches – she was lucky.

On Monday morning, before I left Byron's, I took a call. The voice was barely audible.

"You don't know how much I miss you," it said. "Doing anything today?"

"No, not really."

"Where are you now?"

"I'm on the stairs."

(He never asked.)

"I want to see you as soon as possible."

"Yeah, okay, but I've got to get a job."

"Teaching?"

"If possible."

"Where?"

"A summer school, or maybe a college."

"Nothing much here, not until September."

"Oh? I'm going to ask a friend of mine, the one with the ponytail."

"Let me know if you can meet me in London."

"Okay."

"Bye!"

Byron was in earshot. He was driving me to Kings Cross.

"Honey, I'm home!" Art called. I ran to the door, and then came the high five and the big hug. He always looked immaculate, like a window dresser's dummy. I do not mean that unkindly. His shirts were freshly ironed. Shoes polished. He was almost untouchably perfect. He always travelled business class.

His comings and goings followed a pattern I already seemed to know: Dad's. When Dad returned, he had a signature tap on the inner glass door. It was a kind of percussion to say he was back. One, two, three months he was away. He taught orientation, with a compass, photography, and he detonated bombs.

When Dad came home, he was every inch the wild man, his honey-amber eyes sparkling, his wiry copper hair wind-blown, his high cheekbones, cleft chin, and square, practical hands wind-burnt. My mother used to call him The Spy Who Came in from the Cold. He was the strong, brooding, silent type; popular, but inscrutable. I saw him cry once, alone, at the dining room table.

"What's the matter, Dad?"

He looked at me head on, his face ashen with shock.

"I knew them, they were kids. The boys in Belfast, they were too young."

Whenever the soldiers went on manoeuvres it kept people out. The bombshells were a deterrent, creating a kind of bleak wilderness, a sanctuary for wildlife. When Dad came back, he brought back sketches of kestrels and buzzards, and photographs. And leftover army rations from campfires.

Art brought back stories from the Orient; from Hong Kong, China, and Vietnam. He told me he was planning a holiday to see the guru Anthony Robbins in Arizona. He wanted to do a walk of fire. I think he was seeking a challenge, and excitement.

I cooked a dinner of roast lamb, and opened a bottle of German Riesling, chilled. We talked. We did the washing up together. Then he sat at the computer, by the window, making drawings. I was quiet, reading *To the Lighthouse*. He was inventing something. We could be happy together. We each had our own interests. And when we met up, it was a bigger world.

The Italian was angry at me; I'd been straightforward. It seemed perfectly logical, at least in theory. Art had moved in to help with the rent. I think Antonio thought it wouldn't actually happen. He was docile, warm, caring, and imaginative. I'd never seen him lose his temper. He was so angry he stamped his foot to deliver home the point. He objected in the strongest possible way. We had our only memorable row. I read 'The Rules'. Shameem conspired with me, and when he called she said I was ill, until finally (after a respectable period of elusiveness) I felt calmer, and agreed to see him.

That winter, our first Christmas, we were together. He wanted to keep Art at a distance. He was possessive, and wanted something more; a long-term arrangement. And then the piece of news: "Morley's invited me to a party. Do you want to go, sweetheart?"

"No," I said. I knew what would happen, and someone would get hurt. What were you thinking? Did you know? Did you want to be friends again? I couldn't work it out. I knew I'd leak my feelings for you, unintentionally. Maybe I'd glance a little too long or our eyes would meet full on, and then "Pow!" I wouldn't be able to conceal how I felt about you, or pretend. And if you were with someone, how could I bear to see you with her?

I thought about the time before it all happened. It was winter, and I had Asian flu. My friends from the flats below came to see me. I was trying to write my term papers; maybe I'd have to hand them in late. Mrs Cargeeg from downstairs collapsed, and was taken away in an ambulance. She had watched the world from her window until the day she died: students in their gowns, newly graduated, the gypsy men in the fairground, the football matches, children playing Frisbee and family picnics in the park. I grieved for her. Then Art returned.

I was in my bathrobe; he probably saw me at my least attractive. I took a bath to freshen up.

"Go to bed and rest. I'll bring you a cup of tea, and some supper if you like." He brought me tea at intervals and cold drinks. It was the first time he ever really hugged me. And I was at my worst.

"He cares about me," I told Greta, "and that is part of love, but not all."

I have to admit, at that moment I had a vision of you, parking your car with the 'DOCTOR' sign on the double yellows. You were carrying your black bag, a detached, professional expression on your face, as you climbed the stairway. Greta met you at the door.

"Dr R," you announced, with a quizzical, swift glance, and the familiar fade-out in your voice. The voice seemed to wrap around me, enclose my entire being.

"She's in the bedroom."

Your sensitive hands lightly knocked before you entered. You were a consummate professional. But for me you'd drop formalities. It was the fantasy of all fantasies; even now, it haunts me.

Abroad

Last night, we went to a singing room. Just teachers, no one else. The soldier was practising for the wedding, but he sang other songs as well.

The soundproofed basement room had a mini-bar, a leather sofa, and cushions. Jock took a mike and sang *Stray Cats*. He moved about the stage in a way that confirmed he had once been a commando. I sang a song by Karen Carpenter. I didn't get stage fright as adults sometimes do.

"Why don't you sing a duet," the psychologist suggested.

"What do you wanna sing?"

"Something I know the words to."

We sang *I am a Rock*. There was a frisson of excitement as we sang, "I touch no one and no one touches me." Then the applause, and demands for an encore.

I remember a day on the campus, how furious you were. You returned a book of love poetry in front of my friends. I shouted after you in a fit of temper as you made your escape. You were heading for the medical building, furious I'd skipped your lecture. Rajan, my sparring partner, comforted me over a cappuccino. His dark eyes left me cold. You never knew, I suppose. I should have told you in a song. Music rarely fails to communicate our innermost feelings.

Singing reminds me of my father. I liked to sing at competitions. The big one was the Kathleen Ferrier Memorial Cup. I came in second. Gwynofa Sysiaka won it – she was Polish. But my father was still proud; there were tears in his eyes.

I am the eternal romantic; I hope you'll forgive me for

saying so. Twelve years ago, I had a vision. She was halfway between a woman and a mermaid, her hair flowing as if she came from the waves. An ethereal music invaded my memory. She was standing at the foot of the bed. She did not smile. She seemed to be looking into the distance. She wore a veil, and her gaze was tranquillity itself.

"Don't tell anyone, I want it to be a secret."

In all honesty, I did not understand. I felt that if I touched her, she would have held my hand and spoken. Karen Boxall, the North American from Boston, whose flat was above us, heard footsteps – tap, tap, tap on the floor – when no one was around. I didn't tell her I might have seen a ghost. Perhaps I was only dreaming. I remember the aura that surrounded her from head to toe; it was indigo, the colour of heaven.

They say: "The ghost is the Korean bride and not the drowning woman."

"Suzy, I'm getting married," Elvin said, "and I'd like you to come to the wedding."

"I'd love to come. Where is it going to be?"

"It's in Busan."

"Is it the lovely girl I met when we went to the hospital?"

"Yes," he replied, "but I'm a little nervous."

I smiled. "It'll be okay. Don't worry. I think you've made a good choice."

I thought that they were well matched and made for each other the first and only time I'd ever met her. I went downstairs to the staffroom. It was deserted – no one was doing any prep. A student hovered at the staffroom entrance.

"Elvin is getting married," she said. "Suzy, I'm devastated."

As I re-entered the staffroom, someone was singing; he didn't notice me.

Everyone said he fell in love with her voice before he really knew her. Her major was music, and she was a professional singer. Two weeks before the wedding, the invitation was hand-delivered to my desk. I hoped it didn't require a written reply. I couldn't make out all of it, and opened it later, in the quiet of my apartment. At work the next day I saw the student, the one who was upset. We went to a coffee bar together. She is married, wealthy and miserable. Elvin was her dream man.

"Are you serious?" I said. "He'd be too young for you." I didn't say it was a crush.

"In another life, perhaps we'll be together," she said. "I don't know why he chose her, she's not so pretty. And he says he's thinking to call it off."

"It's nerves," I said. "It's a big decision. Most people have last-minute doubts, it's natural."

"I'm not sure," she said. "He is a rabbit and she is a tiger. You know what they say?"

"That the tiger will eat the rabbit," I said, stifling a giggle. She saw the funny side.

"Nom, nom, nom," she mouthed. It sounded like eating.

"I guess you could have a woman vampire. Elvin cannot be Dracula!" I laughed.

Pearl liked to have men waiting in the wings for her, and if her life was sweet it was because she was the brightest flower. She could sweeten the life of these social butterflies and make them happy. It worked to be desired by many. And now, she was one down. She was at the sort of age where women know what they want and do not need to spread their favours. But something in her nature was coquettish. She enjoyed the uncertainty, the open-endedness of untrodden paths. She had time yet to queen it at the banquet, and if one dish failed to grace her table, there would be yet more.

Some time ago, she'd moved apartments. Her children had flown the nest, one to medical college, the other to military service. She'd be nearer to her elderly mother. It was a kind of separation. She craved company, so she invited Drew, Jock and I over for lunch. She took us there. Her car had a sunroof.

The wind was blowing in our hair. It was kind of fun.

The apartment was on the sixteenth floor, with views of the river. "It's lit up at night," she stated. The lounge was L-shaped, with a chandelier that swung over the glass-top table. The kitchen was well equipped and compact. "I'll show you round," she said.

We peered into the bathroom first. It was a hall of mirrors with a sunken tub and a single toothbrush on the washbasin, which was shaped like a swan. The floor was Italian marble.

In the lobby, there was a baby grand.

We stepped into a bedroom. It wasn't hers. A big round bed filled the room.

"I need someone with burning eyes," she quipped.

And a healthy constitution, I thought.

Drew and Jock sniggered like schoolboys behind her back. I dug my nails into my palms and bit my tongue. "But no one sleeps there," she said, with a touch of longing in her voice. It was the ultimate in anti-seduction, a kind of Venus flytrap. The boys retreated into the living room.

"And this is my room," she said.

It was modern, tasteful and understated. There was a dressing table with silver-topped perfume bottles, a bookcase with English books, and a laptop on the floor.

We returned to the kitchen. I helped her dish up. Jock popped the champagne cork, and Drew dished out the spoons and chopsticks. It was a lovely lunch: pumpkin soup, bulgogi, and salad on the side with a kiwi dressing. The champagne was French Moët. We talked non-stop.

An hour or so passed. Pearl ferried Drew back to work, leaving me and the soldier.

We made small talk as we finished our champagne, and did a walkabout. The blind dog followed us. He was very tactile.

In the lobby, I flipped through the charcoal drawings on the easel. She had a talent for drawing, I observed. Dad used to draw like that in a sketchbook, but his subjects were kestrels, sparrow hawks and eagles, never people.

I tinkled the piano keys. It seemed like years since I'd played, but I hadn't completely forgotten.

"Do you play?" he asked.

"Not anymore," I said. "But I want to take it up again."

"Classical?"

"Yeah, but now I want to play modern stuff with a bit of jazz, like Jools Holland."

He'd spent some years in Britain, so he knew what I was talking about.

"I play guitar a little," he said modestly.

Then the soldier's fingers were strumming some chords. It was a different time and place, and felt like lovemaking. I made an involuntary movement on my lips, answered only by a familiar, quizzical look. I was finding the words – it was *The Shape of My Heart*.

"Do you know the words?"

"Not all, but some of them."

A door opened, invisibly letting her through the gap. I think she was standing there, in a reverie. And he would never stop, playing her, playing with her heart; he was relentless. A photo was what she wanted, and so we complied. But you were there, my lover, you with the curl in your eyelashes. Do you recognise yourself? In a blink I knew I could paint you; it was only a matter of time.

I am walking along a beach in Busan. It's the morning of the wedding. I take a lot of photos these days and I'm not camera-shy. Pearl is with me. She's a small, diminutive woman, with a chiselled face. Like most small women, her childlike demeanour means she's used to being spoiled and getting her own way. But the tide is going out on her life, and life is becoming narrower. She asks me about Barcelona.

"It was good," I say. (But I'll always love the guy with the quizzical look and the quirky mind, the guy with the voice that is powerful and resonant yet quiet and comforting; the kind of voice you hang onto in memory. It soothes, enveloping your heart, in the rise and fall of its cadences, as if to protect.)

"No man is an island," the chubby woman said. (In those days she had been a friend.)

"Are you a psychoanalyst?" (You pause, cautiously. You are in the process of formulating an objective, factual, thought-provoking disclosure.)

I resented the way you engaged with her as an equal; why did I feel like that?

No man is an island, I was thinking. I knew those lines from an ancient poem, and later I saw them, as I studied the preface of a serious tome.

I want to dance with you on the sand when no one else is around – that's what I was thinking. I wanted you for myself. But I'm the kind that has to get it wrong first, that's how I get it right in the end. So what is love? Maybe it's a dangerous kind of knowing.

Sometimes I talk to the spirits, when I am alone, or when in church. Many years ago, at the Holy Trinity back in England, David addressed the congregation.

"The Lord your God is like a lover who cannot wait to come to you."

The church gave me solace. A priest came one day; he was a prophet. He was known all over the world for healing impossible cases and speaking in tongues. I waited in the queue. But Sandra, the pastor's wife, pushed me to the front.

"There's something he's got to tell you," she whispered. "Don't be afraid."

"God is telling you to let go of something that doesn't belong to you," he said. "He's promising you nothing but a blue sky ahead."

I want a blue sky for the young couple. Elvin is a gentle man. I want them to be happy. And I want a happy beginning and ending to the story.

On the day of the wedding, I stood awhile at the water's edge. It is true what they say; it was calm that morning. Pearl and I entered the hotel wedding hall. It was decked with lime green flowers. You could sit wherever you wanted. Elvin came over briefly to say hello. His short jet-black hair glistened under the lights. His skin seemed darker than usual; he was wearing eyeliner. Two video screens showed friends and family every gesture the couple made close-up, as they uttered their vows. The bride looked composed. Her brother sang a song and forgot the words. The wedding guests carried the song to the end. The musicians played *You Raise Me Up.* I thought how true that is of love.

When the ceremony ended, the missionary and I mingled with our colleagues. The usual crowd, DD and his Korean wife, and J were there. It was so relaxed they turned up in shorts. Sarah shone in a white suit, a perfect foil for her long dark hair, and I wore a long cotton dress in green. People said it went with my eyes.

We milled out onto the balcony. The blue seemed to stretch for miles. I thought how brave it was of them, making their vows. I was thinking about the future. A gentle breeze was gathering up, and on the breeze was the faint scent of mimosa.

It was about midday when the gathering dispersed, gradually slipping away this way and that, flowing onto the balcony and onto the beach and into the waiting limousines which glided away, bound for the city and the country. The missionary and I headed for the promenade. We were discussing our future plans. His wife was in remission from cancer, and soon he was heading back to Canada.

Light rippled across the sand. As we were talking, I played

with the warm grains, letting them trickle through my fingers. There were hardly any shells.

"I'm going for a paddle, you comin'?" he said.

I kicked off my shoes and hitched up my dress. I got it wet. The icy shock made me squeal. I found the child in me again. In the distance, J, DD and his Korean wife were coming towards us. DD's wife waved. She had seen my one-piece. The little girl L was in her arms. They came across the sand to join us. She was frightened of the water; it was the first time she had seen it. And she screamed at the sand. Jock took her in his arms and comforted her. He used to be a soldier, but they have a soft side. And then Drew waded out. L knew that Daddy wasn't scared. But when the missionary grabbed Mummy and took her away into the waves, L gave a deafening scream.

"Oh, God," the missionary said. "I've just damaged her for life!"

"I don't think so," I said. "Children are very resilient."

Drew stood by and grimaced. It had touched a nerve with him, I thought.

Borth beach, Wales. That's what it reminded me of. But here the sea was a dark inviting turquoise, a kind of blue nearer the jutting rocks. When the danger flags were out, that's when my mother swam, creating the gap, the distance. My father's heart went out, watching the bombshell sinking. Her silhouette went out: ankles, thighs, hips, waist, and chest. It was treacherous. All you could see now was her head, like a small buoy, just above the briny surface, as the waves crashed. She relished the dance with danger, while my father and I stood motionless and silent, lonely refugees on the sand.

It was Monday morning, the morning after the wedding. I was on the stairs, descending. The soldier appeared. He'd just finished teaching a class.

"Hey," he said.

"Hey," I answered, pausing. He looked intense.

"I've been asked to sing at a wedding," he said.

"Anyone I know?"

"No, they heard me at Elvin's wedding."

"Oh?"

I wasn't surprised – languages and music go together. He was a tenor, but he could sing a phrase with a modern edginess in his voice.

"What are you gonna sing?"

"*You Say it Best, When You Say Nothing at All,*" he replied.

He played with the ring, a jagged edge round his middle finger, handmade in silver.

"D'you think it will be okay for a wedding?"

"I like the song. Are you accompanying yourself?"

"Yeah, I know a few chords. I've been practising." His hands looked sore. "Do you know any love songs?"

It was a throwaway remark. But I knew the game. He was curious. I remembered a song for a breathy tenor voice, a song to dance to nice and slow, in the candlelight. It was a song for lovers who hardly knew each other. I held it close, like a gift. I had it. And he wasn't going to know, so I gave him the substitute.

"*Wonderful Tonight,*" I said. "It's one of my favourites, but if she's Korean, you'll have to sing dark, not blonde."

"Yeah, I kinda like that too," he beamed. "Know any others?"

The smile grew faint and he gave me that quizzical look again.

I laughed. What was it he wanted?

"I'll give it some thought," I said.

The Year of Wearing Black

Last night, I was dreaming of Angela. Everything would be alright, she'd thought. She was walking in a garden of flowers, submerged.

"Angela's killed herself," I said.

I had phoned my mother, in a moment of weakness.

"Dying that way, she would have slowly drowned."

"Not slept?" I said.

I wanted her to sugar-coat the pill, to make it better. But Lillian, my maternal grandmother, had been a nurse, and my grandfather a doctor.

"I'm afraid she would have drowned. The lungs would have collapsed. It would have been a slow, painful death."

People say that when you drown you see a replay of your life in watery pictures; blurry pictures swimming before your eyes, like photos in a developing tray, before they become clear and sharp. I'd had company the night the freemason came. I hadn't known it was part of a net, a trap, and I was being reeled in.

"Don't blame yourself for her death," Gerald said earnestly.

In my dream I made the connection at last. When I heard of her untimely death, my company that evening was telling a mournful tale of how his young wife had drowned.

I sometimes wear the necklace V gave me. I never used to wear it, in case someone asked. My face may have given away the story. But now it's been years; I've come so far since then.

It was the difficult year, the year of crying and wearing black.

I had to collect the keys from the estate agent. Someone

would be down in a minute. I waited. His secretary made a coffee. He'd just come back from Spain. He was so busy, but it wouldn't be long. Would I like another coffee?

"No thanks," I said.

I waited for a man in a suit to come down the stairs from the galleried landing. He'd probably materialise any minute, apologetic, clean-cut and breathless, or else smooth, composed and glib. I imagined he wore a suit, shirt and tie, navy socks and slip-on shoes. But down the stairs came someone refreshingly different; mature, a handsome brute. He was wearing a polo shirt and beige chinos. He had dark eyes, almost black, olive skin, perfect teeth and a cleft chin.

"You must be Sue," he said.

The flat was small, but adequate. I made myself at home. With the stereo on full blast, it was like a capsule. I drank wine almost every day back then, and hardly ate. It was quiet those days. I missed your face. Sometimes I went to the university library, but you were seldom, if ever, there.

One day, I heard the sound of tyres on the gravel. It was V again, with his father, a guy of about seventy-five. They'd come to see me, and was I settling in all right? Then V came alone. He had a teasing laugh in his voice. He told me he'd wanted to go to university, but hadn't, so he'd sold property instead.

"What are you studying?" he said. He was close now, his warm hands on my shoulders as I worked at the table. I turned over the lined pages, put down my pen. He asked if I enjoyed studying.

"I'm taking a year out," I said.

"So you'll have some free time. What are you doing now? Can't you leave it, take a rest?"

If there's such a thing as unlawful carnal knowledge, now I had an inkling of what it meant. The affair ran its course; birthdays, bank holidays and Christmases were lonely. People knew me as the Parisian, because I always wore black. Phillip said they knew wherever I was, V wouldn't be far off.

One day, I suggested that we create space, do our own things, and spend some time apart.

"I'm in love with someone else," I stated simply.

"I told you before, Sue, if you've met someone…or are you still in love with him?"

We knew each other well. I didn't answer; the question seemed to answer itself.

"I'm sorry to let you go. It's been good. It's helped me. Take care," I said.

It seemed so easy to let go this time. But V concealed how he really felt. He wasn't going to lose easily, as I quickly came to realise.

One night, when I got home, the hallway was in darkness. I checked the trip switches, and entered my flat. It was only in the morning I saw the wires had been cut. It was pure vandalism. It wouldn't have been him, surely. I phoned him, and he was happy to oblige. He'd get an electrician, and foot the bill himself. And could we talk things over?

Then there was the nuisance, the man whose wife had drowned. He became a kind of stalker. Late one night, when he was hammering at my windows, V turned up in the nick of time.

"I'll get rid of him for you," he said. And there was never any more trouble. Then V's secretary called to see how I was.

"V's not eating," she said, "and things are getting worse. He's not sleeping in the house. He's not concentrating on his work!"

I knew this spelled trouble; something was wrong. He was a workaholic. He loved the deals. I felt guilty. I began to hate the flat. I decided to move, without saying where I was going. Nothing was right anymore. I cried, looking at the flowers. V had fallen. He hadn't meant to, sometimes it just happens. I should know.

V and his old dad, the three of us, discussed the damage, the possible fallout.

"Leave her for Sue!" he said.

At Christmas, V came to the jewellery stand where I worked.

"This is Daddy's special friend."

Before me stood this adorable little boy. I couldn't build a happy life on someone else's loss. I didn't want him to be a motherless child, with a daddy who had left. I listened to my heart. What a fool I was. I wanted to put things right, make amends, and I needed your insight. I would have to tell him.

I'd packed the boxes. V kept a respectful distance. Then, one day, he called. He was newly suntanned, olive-skinned again. He managed an easy smile.

"Please tell me where you're going, Sue."

"Vicky Park."

He knew where I meant.

"So, can I come round for a cuppa?" he grinned. He had the common touch.

"Just a cuppa, nothing else."

"I won't have time, anyway."

It felt like a reverse kind of psychology. But I feigned I bought it.

"So is business good at the moment?"

"At the minute, there's a market emerging in the Czech Republic, East Germany and Poland. I'm selling my portfolio."

He was his usual self again, and so I relented.

Vanessa

"Hi, is that Vanessa? It's your cousin, Sue."

"Yeah?" She spoke with a rising tone in her voice.

"I'm in deep shit, and I want to come over."

"When?"

"Like tomorrow?"

"Whenever you need. You know I got dogs?"

"How many?"

"Two."

"What kind?"

"Doberman."

"You know I'm scared of big dogs, but I'll try."

"They're all right, I'll take them to Clara's for the night. You drivin'?"

"No. My car's been stolen. I'm coming on the train."

"Are you okay? You don't sound right."

"Not really. I'm fucked. Big time. But I'll get over it."

"What's been goin' on?"

"It's a long story. Tell you when I see you."

"Okay. Meet me at Stoke Newington?"

"You're not in Hackney?"

"Nah. Moved two years ago."

I did know, but somehow I'd forgotten.

"Listen. I've gotta get away from him!"

"We wondered why you didn't come to the wedding."

"Glad I never went anyway!"

"So you've heard they've broken up?"

"No! Just phoned her. Told me she's going on holiday!"

65

"Pam's a bitch! We're not talkin'! She screwed me. Cost me grands!"

"Really?"

"Yeah, believe! What time you comin' over?"

"Can you meet me at five?"

"Stoke Newington? Or we can meet at Notting Hill, but I'll be wiv the dogs."

Somewhat dryly, I said, "Stoke Newington."

"Five – and don't forget, I'll be there if you need!"

"Thanks."

"Cool."

"Bye!"

I wonder if this is the house. I hardly recognised my cousin, her football kit bag slung over her shoulder at the station; so many years had gone. It was a shock to see her face, shrivelled from years of heroin damage, but for some time now she'd kept to her own rehab. Some weed, perhaps, but basically she was clean. We'd always had a liking for each other. And she was my father's favourite out of all my cousins.

I could see her at five, on the floor in the house at Purley. She had a collection of crayons and drawing paper. She drew a picture of a footballer. It was animated, with arms and legs in proportion to the head. Strangely, it was a sophisticated drawing. The art teacher spoke. "That kid's going to be an artist," he said.

The speaker was my father, and he of all people knew. The professor smiled a disappointed kind of smile. I think he wanted her to be a reflection of himself, although she had been adopted. Time proved Dad right – she went to Chelsea Art College. A few years younger than me, she had the opportunity to engage in carpentry and metalwork.

Her house was a reflection of her artistry. Outside was a pottery plaque, which read in Spanish, "Beware of the Dogs!" and a fancy metalwork grille protected the lobby window from break-ins.

Everything in her home she had made with her own hands. There was a mantelpiece made out of oak, and a coffee table made from an old tree, with numerous grainy rings. Various clay pots she had turned on the wheel. Along the stairway family faces gazed down; the photographs were taken by her, and mounted in clip-on frames. I liked the miniature stained glass window most of all.

"You have to be exceptional to make a living," she said.

We stayed up all night, talking, catching up on lost years. She told me she was bi, but I already knew. People had talked. I told her Mina had once made a move; she'd wanted to spend the night and I'd declined – I was heterosexual.

We talked about Doyle; it was difficult to explain.

"I'm fed up with violent relationships," she said.

Her girlfriend had punched her.

"I got her out with a separation agreement."

I admitted I couldn't do the same; I wasn't allowed to disagree, I was there to serve him. I told her about the nights he made me drive to deserted spots and threatened me with his fists.

"I don't know how you got involved. You wouldn't even be friends with someone like that," she said.

"My stepson was dying. I loved him."

Upstairs, Downstairs

"No one else knows?"

"They can't do anything!"

"So, you got no backup?"

"No!"

"I can get you some – it'll cost you, but not much!"

"I don't want to go down that road."

"Welcome to the house of the bitter and twisted!" she said, mock-seriously. "The family never sticks together. But I don't miss it cos I was never a part of that!"

She felt separate, by virtue of her adoption. There'd been her and George that were close.

"He taught me not to give a fuck about what other people thought!"

I could imagine that, and my aunt – she was my godmother, long buried.

"Not as close. Not close at all. Never did what mothers and daughters did together."

"Me too!" I said.

She told me she didn't understand why the distance, why the gap.

"Did you see the picture of the house?"

"Nah."

Vanessa tilted her head like a bird. It was morning now. Her face glowed with the transparency of a pre-Raphaelite. Her skin was like a pale opal against the henna-red of her straight hair. Her eyes were grey, like the sea on a stormy day.

"The house was on the front of *Country Life* once."

My mother had shown me the picture; of this she was more than proud.

"I didn't know that," Vanessa said.

The sisters had led an Upstairs Downstairs kind of life; it was a house with maids and a gardener. They were refugees from the city during wartime. Our grandmother once turned a maid out on the streets for getting pregnant. Our mothers had never known our grandmother well; they were bathed and dressed and had their hair combed by the maids alone.

"Snuggie would have been a shadowy figure climbing the stairs to say goodnight."

At these words, Vanessa sunk back deeper into the faded tapestry chair, casting spliff-ash on the stripped pine floor around her.

"So that is why," she said. "And what about our grandfather?"

"I don't know much," I said.

I'd never met him. He had died before I was born. He was a doctor, but had a temper. The sisters hid under the bed when they were scared of him. He was violent. It was the alcohol. Snuggie endured it, but my mother challenged him. He turned her out with nowhere to go. He died an unhappy man.

"Now it all makes sense," she said, "but I'm not related!"

She thought that Brian and I were survivors; the family was never a haven, and we were different from the rest, but I could feel the chill over the years. My brother was distant; he survived from day to day. One day, my mother nearly passed me in the street. Her eyes were glassy, her vague face expressionless as a piece of frozen meat, her lipstick just missing her mouth, her oversized handbag dangling from her arm, drowning her small diminished frame. She was traipsing the town in search of charity shop finds, things to hoard in her hidey-holes that she could never use, things that filled a well of emptiness.

"What are you doing in my house?"

Realisations about the past. Time lost. Hurt. Regret.

"You look like a broken woman," said my Yugoslavian friend, Nada. She was furious that I'd sunk so low because of a man. But I shook the label off with a laugh, Scissor-Bird.

Today, one of my students is asking me about my writing; the secret is out. I want this book to be a rainbow, to give you hope. There are many colours in black, in the sunlight.

"Is your book about nature?" she asks. "I think it's about beautiful things: the sea and forests and waterfalls and animals and birds!"

She laughs, musically; she sparkles. She wants to fly – that's why I'm helping her. I pause.

"It's about nature, yes, and beauty, and love. It's about human nature, life and so on."

"Are you going to get it published?"

"Probably not."

"I think you should, and I will buy it!" she says, excitedly.

Today, I'm sorry for upsetting you. Maybe you don't like poetry, but not everything is written. I imagine your face: the lift of an eyebrow, the green line of your vision now compelling me to keep silent. It would be easy to click now, and then nothing, words flying off the page, shattering like splinters of coloured glass. Words are like fireflies – they flit about, sculptures lighting the forest, darting between the leaves. From now on, it will be quiet.

Rain

Today is the start of the rainy season. I have mislaid my umbrella. The sky is grey, visibility low. Blocks of steel and white and black shudder to a standstill in the blur of traffic lights. I am wearing orange, yet I am invisible. Maybe I have been here twelve months or so.

Perhaps you are walking along the leafy streets of Kensington or Chelsea. Maybe it is raining there as well. Oblique, cold rain. Or it might be just a shower. I'm there with you, in the shelter of your umbrella. Or maybe you give me your black leather jacket, I put the collar up, and we link hands.

We stop in a doorway, or dive into a bookshop. We separate. I wear my glasses, reading the thrillers. You study the anthropology. And then, as if by chance, we meet up. We pretend not to know each other. I slide the frames thoughtfully down my nose, like the bookshop girl in a black and white movie, and we make eye contact. (I appear to be less bookish without my spectacles.) You say something like: "Well, hello!"

Or maybe you're in Kensington and it's a sunny day. You're on one of your missions. You walk at a pace; you are a shadow, a spectre, a shade of meaning. You seem to look back over your shoulder, but this is rare.

The rain is soft now, my lover, and how I love it; warm globules stroke my face. I am hidden in the half-light, behind the transparency of an umbrella. *Plick, plick, plock*, giant water drops merge with the river. The world is smaller, yet I am enclosed; unreachable, untouchable by others.

I weave between the grainy blocks: black and white and

grey. I am like quicksilver. I zigzag, cut through the parallels like a shape-shifter. I dance and spin through thin air. Catch me... I know you are somewhere, on the tree, the wire, the thread. A vibration, a kingfisher, an ink-blue flash in monochrome.

I thought I heard thunder. Dad and I in a darkroom, on a rainy afternoon, half past three.

"They're ready now."

I lift the emergent pictures from a tray. There's a photo of Big Ben and Trafalgar Square in the rain. I can see the sea and the statue and white horses in the picture. It was a Brownie Reflex camera, and I'd forgotten to wind it on.

A Deck of Cards

He was walking across the small green that led to the bungalows. It was about nine o'clock on a summer's evening. He looked crestfallen. He was lean and agile. On his feet, mod style, were winkle-pickers. His hair was silky and dark, shoulder length. He was wearing a dark green weather-proof mac, jeans, and a plain t-shirt. His upper lip was thin. His cheeks appeared to be hollow. He had a penetrative gaze. His eyes were dark hazel-green, framed by thick, bushy eyebrows. When he lifted his head and spoke in a deep, fruity voice, there seemed to be something incongruent, but I couldn't tell what.

I was babysitting. Her name was Jade. She liked listening to Texas with me. We were playing a game of cards. I could see her from the doorway. I'd only be a minute or two, I said. As I turned my head back again, he was already on the step. His friend Asif was out and he was alone; he'd like to join us.

He was from Robin Hood country. His father was a veterinary surgeon. He was a gentleman farmer, and a civil engineer, and then he had worked to contracts. He had raced cars in Formula 2. I could read the article in the local newspaper if I wanted. He'd been tipped to be as successful as Senna, but the sponsorship had dried up.

He was a good listener, and entertaining. He cheated at cards. He had a sleight of hand I'd never seen before. His face, expressionless, was like a mask; I enjoyed the mystery and the excitement. When he revealed his hand he had the ace of spades. I believe that was an omen.

I talked about riding a horse I used to love called Troy. He told me he had ridden bareback from the age of eight. He had a touch of the Irish about him; I could fall for that.

"The feeling is all in the rear, like driving."

The autumn evenings passed quickly at first in the company of the dark stranger. He talked about the time he went to live in France, and the scent of mimosa reminded him of those romantic days.

St Tropez

I was just twenty-one when I went to St Tropez. I went with some friends; we bought a car and drove.

The rain in Paris was incessant, driving rain; the countryside a little south was still lush. Then near the coast flora and fauna changed; even after the rain the earth was bare and scorched. I could see the sea, dark turquoise, as the car hugged the coastal road. We descended further down, until we reached the caravan park. That night, we had dinner under the stars. We felt tired, and slept in till eleven. Then we headed for the sand.

Sharon told me to take my bikini off. "You won't need it, honest," she said. I wasn't sure; I felt shy and self-conscious. I didn't want to undress in front of strangers.

"Just pretend you're at the doctor's," she suggested. That seemed to make it worse.

"I'll decide when I get there," I said.

It was the girl with the boob job that gave me confidence. Bartholomew admitted he couldn't help staring; when she went horizontal, her breasts stayed pert. Anything goes, I thought, so I peeled my black and pink bikini down to my ankles.

The sun was my lover; I surrendered to tendrils of heat. There was the swell of the sea in the distance, the rhythm of the waves. My heart joined in the rhythm, surfing the waves. I was riding a rollercoaster, each wave coming faster, a little faster than before, and larger than the first. In life and in lovemaking, it's all in the timing. This one was going to be big. I thought I was falling in love again. I was serene. Next time, you will make the running. I know you'll plan it, to the last detail. I'll be at my finest; one of the beautiful people. There's no one else who comes close.

The holidays in France were halcyon days. Bartholomew and I went sightseeing, taking the car along the coast to Port Grimaud where Peter Sellers had a flat, although we never saw him. Sharon and Nigel wiled away the hours sunbathing. We picked them up at around six and exchanged stories.

Sharon and I spent evenings exploring narrow cobbled alleyways with high class boutiques. I enjoyed practising my schoolgirl textbook French, chatting with the locals. Sometimes they said, "Do you come from Paris?" and I felt somewhat flattered. When I saw the way those ladies dressed, their understated elegance, I wanted to be them. Once, we caught a glimpse of Bardot – she was gorgeous.

Sharon and Nigel were blondes, and dressed in a studied casual style that was *de rigueur* for sports stars: all in white, with sweat bands on their wrists and heads, and Ray-Bans. (Bartholomew and I secretly joked about that, calling them poseurs.)

The evenings were my favourite time. The little town sparkled like Van Gogh's *Starry Night*. There was colour and vibrancy. I loved people-watching. There was music. It was a fantasy floating world of beautiful strangers.

We sat outside a restaurant or intimate bar, the sun sinking slowly down into the blue of the ocean. People in Pohang do the same. On New Year's Day they gather on the beach, muffled against the Siberian wind, and the sun rolls down, a burnished jewel in a steel hand, and everyone takes photos.

"Let's go to America next year," Bartholomew said.

I thought of dear old Dad, who loved the Big Easy. One of his favourite radio programmes had been 'Letter from America'.

Challenges

These days it's a struggle. But I am the one who ran – a long distance cross-country runner. The order was always the same. I was third, out of sixty. Jane Webb and Alison Cherry always beat me. Jane was lithesome, like a whippet. Alison was strategic. I was heavier than average, but my legs were long. I was stubborn, the sweat dripping down my forehead till the ringlets were sticking to my head, rivulets streaming down the small of my back, my feet sticking to my socks, and my skin rosy-hot, my heart pumping in my throat till it burnt. I could see the ribbon and my father's face. I could tell him it was nothing, just a jaunt across the fields for fun.

When things are difficult I think of that. Or sometimes I ride my favourite horse, Troy, the first horse that ever took me to full gallop. He had a white star on his forehead. His hair was almost black, like jet. I didn't ever take a formal lesson. My grandmother, who had been a farm girl, said, "She only needs you to explain before the trek – it's in her blood see!"

But it was the horse that showed me. It knew a novice rider.

In my dreams, in these dark days of shadows, I am Rhiannon, flying on my white horse with a black star on its forehead, and I am 'The Maker of Birds'. I want to be your night-rider, thundering through the skies till birdsong, and the touch of the sun.

The Joker

Stephen enters the staffroom, singing; he's got an arrangement with his wife. It's open, he's happy. Maybe it's the tall one, with the bangs. She always wears shorts. I don't judge these days.

"Hey, Steve," I say, casually. "Good night?"

"Yeah, but quiet. It's interesting, the link between sex and religion, isn't it?"

His smile is gappy, playful. I'm in one of my controversial moods.

"Well, in both cases you're on your knees," I reply. He's laughing now, but it's not so shocking.

I have a vision of a temple, your body, and my confession. There is incense burning, and you are behind the curtain. If I draw it back now, what will happen?

I play the joker, the one-liner, the quick return. But they'll never know. Didn't I ever tell you? You make my heart light. You send me. With one look from you, my spirit soars.

The Shaman

I want to see a shaman, I decided. She was in a Buddhist temple, the other side of town.

I went with one of my students. The shaman is his aunt.

We ring the bell. She takes time to answer. We slip off our shoes and climb the three steps.

She's a short, curvy woman, with brown, almond-shaped eyes and jet-black hair, piled up in a bun. Her chin is small and pointed. Her ears are large with generous earlobes. She's wearing a string of iridescent pink pearls. She pours tea. My student translates.

"What is it you want to know about?"

"Whatever is important?"

"There are spirits around you, especially your father. He's standing behind your left shoulder. He's with you now!"

I recoiled at the choice of the word shoulder, but then there was more.

"Why am I seeing a body?"

"I'm not sure."

"Are you writing something?"

"Well, yes, kind of."

"You need to write it to help someone. Someone is going to help you write it."

That could be true, I thought. Sometimes, when I write, it is like flying a plane on autopilot; it takes you over, it becomes automatic.

She did not use the Tarot; she went into a trance. Her face transfigured into something innocent. The knowing flew from her deep eyes. She was singing in tongues.

"Why is she singing?"

"They are!"

"Who? Ask her!"

"The children!"

"Why?"

"You write as if someone is singing."

She was smiling now. She took off the string of pink pearls.

"These are for you!" she said.

She wrote some Hangul on a piece of paper, and wrapped the parchment in red silk with gold characters. She told me that she had written me some prayers.

"This will give you protection when you travel."

She wanted to give me a tour of the temple. She could tell I loved music.

"Come this way," she said.

She'd been an opera singer when she was younger. There were pictures of her sitting at the piano; pictures of her holding glittering trophies in a blaze of lights; pictures of her with the former president, Roh Moo Hyun, at the Blue House. He had consulted her, as had celebrities, from the stage and screen.

The temple was decorated with orchids. Otherwise, it was simple. The floor was lacquered pine. We returned to the low table and drank green tea from earthenware cups.

"There's a man you love," she said. "And he's a gentleman. Does he write as well?"

"Yes," I said. "He's written many books."

"I think he's very interested in medicine," she said, "and you have a spiritual connection with him."

"What do you mean?"

"You understand each other."

"I don't see him these days."

"You will see each other in the future," she said.

I didn't ask her when. She is known to be the wisest woman in Daegu.

The Silver Screen

My advanced class talked about films today. I taught them the British version.

"I like films!"

"I like the cinema."

"I like going to the pictures."

I can't resist a piece of nostalgia: "I used to like going to the flicks when I was a kid."

They ask me what films I like – a big question. I tell them I'm out of touch. I only like the old ones these days. I like the ones they used to make, real films, such as *The Great Escape*, *The Killing Fields*, *Schindler's List*, *The Bridges of Madison County*, *The Witches of Eastwick*, *The Italian Job*, *Dead Poets' Society*, *It's a Wonderful Life*, *The English Patient*, *The Big Sleep*, *Casablanca*, *Vertigo*, *Ryan's Daughter*, *Scent of a Woman*, *The Sound of Music*, and *My Fair Lady* – a mixed bag.

I tell them I don't like *Trainspotting* or *Shallow Grave*.

"Do you like animation?"

"Yes, it's clever."

(I've described the little flick-book I had with my father's drawings of a ballerina; that's how animation started.)

"What's your favourite animated film?"

"*The Snowman.*"

"Why?"

"It's about flying. I like the soundtrack. If you don't blink, you can see aerial views of Brighton."

Suddenly, I thought of you, in passing. They are engrossed now, in a group. I can do two things at once, almost blindfolded.

It was only when you moved I noticed how beautiful you are. I can still hear your voice, feel the pace of it. It is the kind of voice that trains the ear to listen. Your eyes are wet and magnetic, scanning the sea of expectant, studious faces. Your gaze alights on the far wall, and then the front row, by the window. I am looking out at the snow. Aware of your presence in front of me, I refocus. You capture my attention. Behind me, I hear the hum of voices.

"Well, now, are you ready to start?"

There were moments of stillness. Your eyes looked and listened, seeming to answer a question with a question, so one made discoveries. You were simply wonderful. You knew your art. I can see now the shy nod, the sudden laugh that lit up the portals to your deep soul.

This is how I remember, flicking through the film of moving pages. The soundtrack is dubbed, catching up with the gestures. I make editor's cuts. Memory is selective.

"When he looked that way, what did he say?" I ask them.

"When he said that, what did he mean?"

What actor could possibly play you? I could be methodical about it, list your qualities. But the whole is more than the sum of its parts.

The Graduation Ball

Autumn is my favourite time of year. For me, it means beginnings; the wind, firelight, the rain in your hair. Reflections in your eyes, like mirrors. Fireworks. Most of all, a slight chill in the air that lets people get close. It's difficult for fathers and daughters; displays of body contact can be misinterpreted, unless they know who you are.

Autumn came early one year at the start of summer. It was the graduation ball. Art would be away in Arizona: Anthony Robbins – the fire walk. Antonio encouraged me to see my friends; he'd be in Italy with his sons. These days the others had cooled off, but Greta would be there. I was writing a letter – two things at once.

"I wish I could see you in that dress," Art said.

The gown was black, long, with ruffles at the shoulders. The shape was hourglass, but I didn't want to show him yet. It was unusual for him; call me naive, others have, but I didn't know he saw me as a woman. When he said, "I've never dated anyone striking before," I wondered. 'Striking' – that was my word for my dad, so I was like him. But 'dated'? What was Art thinking of? I made a joke of it, maybe even flirted, with a sideways glance.

"You're not so bad yourself," I said.

I knew what it was: he wanted to boost my confidence. Just like Art to lift someone up and be positive, pay them a compliment; maybe this was the effect of having a life coach. He demanded a dress rehearsal, but I was too shy.

"I'll show you some other time," I said.

He had dazzling blue eyes, but was solemn now, sitting

at the computer. Why did I always write things by hand? He'd teach me anytime. I told him about my technophobia. I couldn't work with computers; they were alien.

"Writing is an intimate act," I said. "You write with the body."

The graduation ball came. There were hardly any sociologists. It reminded me of fresher's week. We went into the Percival building where we drank copious amounts of beer, then helped ourselves to pizza.

There was a firework display. We stood behind the barriers, at the back of the crowd. Greta's face glowed. The light played across her small, round, affable pixie face and caught the blonde in her soft, light brown hair. She was telling me about her lover, the one who worked for the Samaritans. He was getting keen on her, but she kept him guessing. And how was the Italian?

"He's simpatico," I said elusively. I felt self-conscious and played with a wisp of my hair.

"You could do a lot worse," she said dryly.

A mature couple nearby were lost in each other, gazing into each other's eyes, and engaging in the grunts and moans and murmurs that gain implicit meaning and are only understood between them over time.

"Oh, it's not like that," I laughed, "and anyway," I added, "there's someone I'm still in love with."

Greta smiled wryly. "Mm, yes," she said.

The fireworks were sophisticated. Hundreds, I thought, maybe thousands, up in smoke. These days I question the extravagance. What purpose does it serve? Maybe I'm old, but there's a lot about life like that; sometimes it's absurd.

The Catherine wheels were my favourite, white dazzling lights, spinning round like stars, reaching outwards in clusters, moving in a curve; circular, not linear, like time. Then there was the finale. A minute remnant of rocket came down, singeing my hair. It was a baptism of fire.

"Let's get some more beer," Greta said, leading the way.

We danced among pieces of broken glass in the Percival building, shouldered our way through boisterous crowds. We hung around in drink queues. When we left, it was 1am.

It was drizzling in Victoria Park. I was on Exmoor. What dangers lurked there?

Greta's dress was knee length. She took her killer heels off, I gathered up the taffeta, and we ran, shrieking like children into the abyss. My flat had moved. Had some trouble with the door keys; it was the neighbour's. Then I found my own front door.

The staircase was impossibly cruel. So far to climb. But we were nearly at the top now, and we cleared the inner door. In the lounge the carpet was lifting; it was the wind blowing under the boards. We stayed up late.

At 11am, Greta surfaced, her face expectant, her bedhead hair casual. She was wrapped in a soft white cotton dressing gown. Greta languished at the table, making slow, circular movements with her unvarnished toes as she tore apart a warm croissant. She phoned her lover. At twelve, a bell rang; it was her husband.

"Don't drive," he said. "I'll take you back."

Our eyes met, I kissed her soft face, and down the stairs they descended. Their voices blended into an echo, a murmur. I ventured barefoot into my bedroom. The dark gown lay crumpled upon the bed.

Ties That Bind Us

"Honey, I'm home!" Art said.

"Yeah, it's good to see you!" I replied, jumping up and down in the hall.

It gave me a thrill to see him back safe, and I had so much to tell him: the graduation ball, the Italian, and how I missed you. We had dinner that evening, some fancy Italian dish with chicken and cheese and wine sauce. He didn't mind being the guinea pig and giving me his honest verdict. And I'd got a few beers in; finally he'd admitted he didn't care for wine.

"The fire walk was awesome," he said. "The power of the mind is greater than you think."

I told him I'd always thought it was glamorous he'd been to Arizona, China and Hong Kong.

"What about the business trip?" I asked.

He looked coy now. He pulled out some photographs.

"This is someone I just met – she's a waitress."

She looked about twenty. Studious, with glasses.

"Is she a student?"

"No. But I think she wants to come to Britain."

"So are you going to keep in touch?"

His arm crossed over his body, he adjusted his tie.

"We're just friends."

"No romance, then?"

"No, but we're keeping in touch," he said decisively.

Last night, I dreamt I was flying. It was the Scottish crew, headed up by Captain White. He always rigged the crewing so we'd fly together. He was a one-off – he had his plans. At the start of the season, I asked him where he lived.

"I've got a stud farm," he said. "I'll fly you over it if you like – you can sit in the cockpit."

(It was crew only on the plane.)

I remember flying over Uffington; he flew just low enough to see the white horse. I imagined what an aerial view would be like if it were luminous. It would be like going into free fall, riding the skies on Pegasus' wings.

Two weeks under a Cypriot sun. The crew lazed by the pool, swimming and sunbathing, drinking cocktails, partying till dawn.

"You can go wherever you want!" the captain said.

So I took myself off, alone, on the coastal road, and joined the others when the sun rolled down, a tangerine into the azure.

The return journey took me to The Land of My Father. A voice came over the airwaves. Out of the starboard window, I could see a rainbow and the metal of an approaching craft.

"Och, we're gonners!" someone breathed.

The oxygen masks were about to descend and then we shot up. My eardrums hurt. The press never reported it. Only crew heard. The captain marched to the tower.

"It's a training ground," he said, "loss of contact, lack of backup!"

His cool seemed to have evaporated into thin air.

The debriefing was short. We stuck to essentials. We bonded. No need for words. Fear sometimes instils loyalty. Scary movies, roller coaster rides; I've heard people often fall in love on planes.

"There aren't any old-fashioned bars left," I said.

But he found one, with a jukebox and real ale. The moon glowed like a galleon in the sky, and I was high, high up on his shoulders. We ran through the night, along rainy passageways, surf cascading onto granite, beating through the barriers, wind whistling round the darkest corners. In awe, we listened to the swell of the waves as the gulls spun silently around above us. We looked up to the firmament in wonder. Captain White's lips tasted of the sea. I clung to him, my arms around his neck. I felt lucky to be alive. I felt safe, thank God.

The Stargazer

"How about coming to midnight Mass?" Art said.

Shameem was fascinated; an Indian shoemaker's daughter, she'd been to temples, but never church. My Irish cousins told me people were often drunk before services. The church was called St James's. It was just across the park.

When I saw the candles, firelight flickering across the angelic faces, I wondered if there might be a higher power, a mystery to it all. The priest spoke to the congregation; his voice was low and rhythmical. A heavy aroma of incense pervaded the building, and the organ began to play. The choir sang, almost in one voice, and I could feel my eyelids begin to close.

I'd sooner be at Stonehenge, I thought, or in Giza, in Egypt. The pyramids were an ancient kind of clock that charted the movement of the stars and planets. Maybe I'm a romantic, but when I look at the sky, I feel how small I am, how insignificant, and I know there must be some higher power behind the grand design.

I followed Art's gaze as his eyes flew from the altar to the candles to the choir. As we left the church after the service, I saw him make the sign of the cross. He was a deeply religious man, and he liked stargazing; he had a telescope.

"What did you think of the church?" I asked Shameem.

She didn't believe in organised religion.

"Yes, it's secular," I agreed. "It's about God, but not of God. I believe in following my faith."

It was one of our evenings in 'the garret', as I dubbed it, although it wasn't really an attic. We talked about arranged marriages, and how Indians believe you can learn to love by being close.

The first time I ever went to a theatre alone was on my first day in Reddington at The Hayloft. It was the story of Sita and Rama in exile. None of the singing was English, it was all in Gujerati. I wanted to see if I could understand. The gestures of the body were my signs. A story was unfolding of good versus evil and the power of love.

One day, in the museum, I took some textile workers to a fabric exhibition. It would expand their vocabulary, give them fluency practice. As we explored the artwork, I noticed a collage. I pieced the story together and arrived at an ending without examining the whole. I asked a student if it was the story of Rama and Sita.

There was silence. Then one of the students spoke.

"It tells the story of lovers, in the forest. But it's a story of shame as well. It's about a family who are disowning their daughter. They are capturing her and killing her to keep the family's honour. She won't marry who they want, innit." As he speaks, his eyes are fixed on me as he rolls his head from side to side. The effect of this is that I know he is sincere.

"Is it a true story?" I whisper.

A tall young man next to me makes a thoughtful clicking noise with his mouth. After a few minutes of deliberation, he decides to speak up: "Yes, women in India are burned alive, even today."

Two more students, one nudging the other, have something to say. The older one speaks up for both of them. "They pour petrol on them. They take them to the country…"

I reflect on a secret studier, one I taught, whose family never knew.

"Don't post me my certificates," she pleaded. "I'm going to change my identity, get myself a better life."

Gita was going to university against her family's wishes.

Elaine said it was a quiet revolution. Now that was romantic. But she wasn't the only one.

"Is it really as bad as that?" I asked Shameem.

"Yes," she said.

Her parents had found her many different suitors, but she'd turned them down, one by one. They'd almost given up. But they were not traditional. She was lucky. They agreed that through her education, they were teaching her future daughters too.

"I was born a shoemaker's daughter," she told me, "I'm supposed to marry someone of my own cast. That's my fate. The next cast down to shoemakers are the untouchables." She had a degree, and a masters; she refused to marry below her level. "I'm not marrying anyone," she said, "unless they can match that, or better!"

I must confess, I didn't know what I thought then, but I do now. You see, men sometimes hit women of superior intelligence to them, or women who earn more money than they do, or women who are breadwinners; it's their way of bringing them down. I think there's evidence, some people say, if you look closely enough.

The story of Sita and Rama is a magical story of a woman who walked on burning coals to prove her innocence and purity. Some people say it takes courage, and the power of the mind.

Just a Number

"My brother's coming down from Manchester, with his girlfriend," Art said. "She used to be an air stewardess, like you were. How about coming to the Spanish restaurant with us on Saturday night?"

"I'd love to," I said, "as long as we go Dutch."

He waved his hand as if to refuse. "No," he said. "I want your company. I'll pay – it's my turn. You've cooked loads for me!"

I hesitated. I'd broken up with the Italian, but Art said he'd met someone. I'd seen the photos. She looked sweet. I told myself not to be silly. It was my imagination again. He liked me for being a good person. He didn't mean anything else, I was sure of it.

"Say you will, Sue, please," he said, fixing his gaze at me.

"Well, alright," I said, gazing back at him.

I told Greta about it later, on the phone.

"Do you find him attractive?"

"Yes, in a low key kind of way. But he's too young. I need an older man, with experience, who can protect me."

"I think he'll ask you out soon," Greta said.

"The stakes are too high," I replied. "What if it all goes wrong, and then I'd lose a friend?"

I must confess, you were there, in my thoughts. I wasn't looking for someone to be my father, just someone like him; someone with sensitivity, someone to be my steadfast friend, someone who aroused my passions, someone I could love wholeheartedly, someone with a voice that I could love, as if I were blind.

I remember that night at the Spanish restaurant, the one in the student quarter, with unruly spider plants on the upstairs balcony; they were grown in old lavatories used as pots. Art was dressed smart casual, his air was relaxed. We sat upstairs. Then, after we'd ordered, a bevy of beauties were climbing the stairs, right next to our table.

One of them was wearing a short black dress that showed off her incredible bronze cleavage. Her best friend wore one in shocking pink silk. They looked like gifts, birthday presents. Art's blue gaze followed the direction of the group; one of them was straightening her skirt as they waited to be seated at a nearby table. He caught me looking, too.

"Those women are nothing when compared to you!" he gushed.

He and his brother exchanged a look. My skin prickled with an admixture of self-consciousness and pleasure. He'd said it out loud, in company. But I couldn't love him in the way he wanted. Maybe, just maybe, it was an eloquent compliment – I hoped so. I decided to ask a girlfriend.

"Don't forget it's Mother's Day soon!" I reminded Art, flagging up a date on the calendar in the kitchen. I was always mindful of occasions – they meant a lot to me.

"When?" he said, standing at the kitchen doorway. And then, for confirmation, he went to check the calendar; he needed to see things.

"Sue," he said slowly. "I haven't contributed anything in the way of furniture to this place – is there anything you need? How about a Welsh dresser?"

"The floorboards wouldn't stand it," I said, "but I could do with a long cupboard to store the china, one that would double as a work surface."

He wanted to act on it immediately that morning. "Yeah, let's," I said. We wandered down New Way and past the Firebird Arts Centre, to a store with antique furniture.

"Have whatever one you like," he said, running his fingers along the parquetry and examining the quality. He added, "But promise me you won't fight over it if we get divorced!"

A sales assistant was standing behind a makeshift counter, her arms folded, an expression of quiet desperation disappearing as Art winked at her.

Then there was the Mother's Day card, tossed aside, with the envelope written in Art's precise hand. I couldn't help noticing it had 'To Mum, with Love from Both of Us' printed on the front. The card only had his signature. It was so unlike him to be careless. I couldn't believe he'd forgotten it, so I asked him.

"Does it say from both of us?" he said. His blue eyes shone in my direction. "I didn't notice!"

"I thought you had a girlfriend," I replied. (I felt like the third party.)

"No," he said, "I told you we were just friends!"

He was reading a tabloid at the breakfast table. He spoke the words into the pages, and then, looking over the paper, searched my face again.

The big gesture left me with a hollow feeling in the pit of my stomach. I couldn't afford the council tax.

"Here's a thousand," he said. "It's nothing to me – pay the council, and spend the rest on what you want!" He talked with his hands outstretched.

I challenged him; I only wanted to borrow it.

"We're family, right?" he said. "I won't accept it if you try to give it me back. If you really want to return it, put it into an orphanage or use it to help children!"

All of the above I presented to Greta as evidence that he was a really brilliant friend.

"I think he's in love with you!" she said.

I could tell she liked the idea; I could hear the German in her accent.

"But he's eight years younger than me," I protested.
"So?" she said. "Age is just a number!"
"I know that one!" I said.

Losses

Maybe my first love was my father, and only you matched up. I think intelligence is sexy. Sometimes, men don't. And that's the problem: you play dumb. My world crumbled when I lost him.

I remember our last detailed conversation. He always found it easier to talk when we were alone, to avoid my mother's jealousy, the inevitable tug-of-war. She always had to win. A middle child, she specialised in that; she was unsure of her position, and carried it into adulthood.

We were in the VW, on the way to my piano lesson with Mrs Cross. It came as a shock; he dropped it so casually, so plainly.

"I don't know how long I've got to live. I'm rattling with pills. I don't feel my usual self these days. I want you to know I love you, whatever happens. Promise me you'll look after your mother and your brother, if, well, what I mean is, if I die."

"You'll be okay, Dad," I said naively.

"I don't feel well," he repeated.

"Dad, I want you to see a doctor!"

"I have, and I don't want them to carve me up. It's my heart, the angina. I can hardly breathe sometimes. I think I'm beginning to lose my memory." (So that was why we often played Kim's Game.)

I was just a kid. What could I do? I couldn't hug him; he was driving. Maybe for him that would be too much, so he hid behind the wheel. The GP was a personal friend of his. He'd told him he wouldn't go privately; he'd queue like anybody else on the NHS.

"Don't mention anything to your mother yet," he said.

I nodded, fighting back the inevitable tears. I worshipped the ground he walked on.

Mrs Cross was her usual cheery self.

"Anything the matter? You're not the Susannah with the smile I know!"

I asked to go to the lavatory.

When I came down, my mascara smudged, I managed to keep it to myself. Sometimes she talked with my mother.

The music for that week was *Für Elise* and *Moonlight Sonata*. I played as well as I could. And as I played, I had a vision: someone was sleeping; I thought it was my father.

I'd often asked him if he believed in God. He used to tell me he didn't know. I'd often asked him, before I knew how ill he was, what happens after you die. "I don't know, maybe nothing," he'd say. He liked facts and science. He was unusual for an artist; he didn't care for speculation, he wanted evidence. When he sketched a bird, or a mountain, it looked like a photograph. He represented things as they were.

Then the day came: four o'clock in the morning, March the thirty-first, Walsgrave Hospital, Coventry. I was with him.

"My little girl," he said, "it's not a bad day today."

As he fought to get the words out, a seagull came inland, and on white wings he was borne away.

On the journey home, the sun shone through the elms which lined the road. The leaves were in bud; soon the branches would be clothed in green, and the mornings light, and the evenings long. How sad to die when nature was about to renew. The trunk of the magnolia tree, a wedding present from my grandmother, was cleaved in two and charred. In autumn, a lightning bolt had struck. There would be no more blossoms. My mother told me of the gypsy's curse which lasted for eight years, maybe more.

No more lifts to school. It wouldn't matter if I played T Rex too loud. No compliments if I looked nice. Or, "Joan, teach her how to put on makeup!" if I disappointed him. There was no one listening, as far as I was aware, as I fumbled a plodding tune at the piano. No trips to Wales, just Dad and me, and the illicit fry-ups at transport cafes on the way. No talks about the Sorbonne, his dream for me, and what the future might hold. No sweets when I got late prep for failing at mathematics again. No sound of his tender voice.

I glimpsed my mother's profile – she was still quite beautiful, but sad now, a widow at forty-nine. What would people say? I could see the shadow of a bird-woman, her body frail under the weight of the news. Then there was the little blonde boy with dark brown eyes, just seven, eight years my junior; he didn't know anything.

How awful, if one of Dad's friends didn't hear, and then they called. (He had lots of names because he was many things to many people; it was not affectation, contrivance, or subterfuge. They were all his names; his life had been full.)

"Is John there?", "Is Jack there?", "Hello, Suzy, is Ronnie there?", "Hello, Sue, is Ron there?" Or even, "Can I speak to Ronnie the Red?"

That afternoon, we collected my brother from the neighbours, and when we'd been home a few minutes he asked, "Where's Daddy?"

I was sitting on the stairs; he was in the hall. My mother's step followed mine. I looked back.

"I'm going to say he's on holiday," she whispered.

I was horrified. "You can't!" I said.

"I'll say he's ill, for the time being, and let him down gently," she said.

I stuck rigidly to my point of view.

"You can't," I said.

"I can't tell him!" she pleaded.

"But you've got to!" I insisted.

"Where's Daddy?" the voice said again.

My mother's eyes flew to mine; she was shaking her head.

"If you don't want to say it, I will."

"Okay."

My mother's head nodded. I bit the bullet. I remember, in those few split seconds I ran through the alternatives, and how they sounded to a child. "Daddy's gone to sleep." (Maybe he'd think he'd wake up.) "Daddy's gone to sleep and won't ever wake up." (Maybe he'd want to see him happy and sleeping.) "Daddy's passed away." (Too sophisticated.) "Daddy's dead." (Didn't explain the process.)

Now I had it. "Julian," I said softly. "Come here, that's right, good boy. I'm really sorry, Daddy has been very ill. He's died, I'm sorry." Instinctively, he raised his arms above his head as if to reach for someone. Then his eyes squinted as the tears escaped. As they tumbled, he resembled someone who had awakened abruptly, and who now looked at something all too bright, all too stark. I bit back my tears, the tears that never came, except in solitude, in secrecy. My brother was in my arms. I hadn't wanted to be the messenger of doom. Perhaps he would blame me, hate me for this forever. My mother stood back. And finally, she went to him.

Quietly, I climbed the stairs up to my room. I adopted the foetal position, put my arms around myself, and closed my eyes. I could still hear the voice, which sounded English, if not for the slight lingering on the l's and the lilt when he was emotional. I would miss him.

He didn't say, "Honey, I'm home," he just said, "Hi, I guess you're Sebastian."

(I'd asked him about this summer arrangement, to which he'd agreed on the phone.)

Sebastian was a history major. He was sharp and humorous and he had a very good memory. He seemed older than his years. We'd gone to a dance in the Czech Republic. We liked each other; he liked Anne Bancroft. And I wanted to take my mind off you.

But males are territorial, in a way I hadn't understood before. Sebastian was arty. He put a red lampshade in the kitchen, and a red light bulb.

"It looks like a brothel!" Art said.

Then they disagreed about music; Art turned The Stones down. Sebastian complained about Art's antique wardrobe; it was hideous. I played the peacemaker, treated them fairly. But then one day, when Sebastian had had an argument with me, Art approached me when I was alone.

"He's even younger than I am!" he said.

Art wanted him out. I thought of the lonely nights I would have, and his lovely mother who was a friend, so Sebastian was going to remain.

I can still see Art hurriedly packing his bags on the landing. I kissed him goodbye. He loved me, and I had missed the obvious. I wish we were still friends. Platonic relationships are impossible, or rare.

Bohemia Revisited

He lived in a Victorian terrace, although they now call them cottages, not far from my flat and the park.

"Alright?" he said, leaning on a door frame. He was wearing bleached denim jeans, a bright blue and pink patterned shirt, and a neckerchief with tassels. He had a single earring, and his ponytail was beaded, with elastic bands at the end.

In the centre of the lounge was a dark wooden coffee table on which there stood an illuminated globe of the world. There was a bookcase with some works of Nietzsche, a copy of *Das Capital*, an *Everyman's Guide to the Law*, and a well-thumbed book on A-level sociology in the alcove. In one corner of the room was a large terracotta vase with peacock feathers and an oriental fan. There was no television. There were several Moroccan wall hangings, and an Indian rug on the yacht-varnished wooden floor. At the kitchen entrance was a computer.

I took a seat. He engaged in conversation as he worked, his back facing me.

"I thought you wasn't comin'," he said.

"I was writing a poem."

He swivelled the office chair round, took a drag on a sweet-smelling cigarette and said,

"Are you ready? Want to see something?"

He produced the poem he'd just written for a new conquest.

"What's it about?"

"Different roads; ley lines."

The words were ornate, and I giggled at the choice of flowery language.

"How about the businessman, the property developer?"

"I think he's having me followed – a guy on a bike, with leathers."

"You don't 'alf pick 'em. Why would 'e do that?"

"Obsession. Control. To turn me on."

"Go on, admit it, you're a leather fetishist, Suzi Quatro!"

"Not exactly," I said. "But if you mention size nines, or tongues, or Italy, or Nancy Sinatra, well, now you're talking!"

We both laughed and laughed.

"Do you like 'Venus in Furs'?"

After the fooling around, I became serious.

"Sure," he said. "The Head of Department is Coller – she's Welsh."

I hit it off with Coller right from the start. She gave me a tough interview, to see if I measured up.

"Your CV spoke to me," she said, and offered me the job.

Words, I thought; she was a linguist with a modern languages major. They meant a lot to her, too. Of course, Phil had said that he knew me, as a favour, but I doubt if that alone had persuaded her.

When the college expanded, and the paperwork, I remember how she looked bureaucracy in the face and dealt with it. The inspectors were coming, and there was still more administration. It was hurriedly completed – we liked teaching.

"What they don't know won't hurt them!" she chirped, spilling bulging files behind a metal cabinet, and closing it up against a wall. "Perfect, innit!"

The Welsh say 'innit' as a universal tag, just like Gujerati speakers. It was all about ley lines, Phil thought; the entire English as a Second Language department had 'the Welsh connection' and we were only four.

One day I told Coller I was going to South Korea. I'd set my sights on an MA at Sussex, on the Downs by the sea.

"I'm going home, to Swansea," she told me, "to the valleys."

We said our goodbyes in an Irish pub.

"I'll miss Coller," Phil said afterwards. "She was a rebel."

I thought so as well; she called a spade a spade.

Nice Work

Sebastian and I were history; we'd had five good years. Passion had faded into friendship, and we agreed to call it quits. I'll go back to Reddington, I thought. I needed somewhere to live.

"Rent my flat!" V said on the phone. "I'd love to see you again!"

It fitted in with my plans, hand in glove. The timing seemed right. I wanted to agree, so I did. But I hoped I'd see you in the leafy streets of Shelley Park. "How's it going?" you seemed to say. Maybe we'd go for a walk. All I needed was the right place, the right day, a second chance, and you'd gather me up in your arms, and this time it would be as it was meant to be: a relationship between equals, or just about.

On a warm, sunny day, I went to see Carlos. His reputation went before him; he was urbane, sophisticated, although I hadn't studied him that closely the first time we met. I knocked at the door with some trepidation. Before me was the contemporary man. He swivelled a leather chair round to greet me. He had the air of a demi-god in a white room. It was on an upstairs floor.

His desk was immaculate. He had a photo on it in a silver frame. It was a picture of his son, Sol; it rolled off the tongue when he said it out loud.

He was dressed completely in white. His face was tanned. His dark blonde hair was spiked and gelled. My eyes glimpsed his feet. They were small for a man, and on them, white tooled-leather Spanish sandals; I could see the skin of his toes and the soles of his feet through the fine leather straps. He just wanted to deal with the details, he said.

"So what new ideas are you going to bring to E.S.O.L?" His eyes twinkled when he smiled.

"I think I'll teach some classes through music, through songs."

"What kind of songs?"

"Anything with good lyrics, which people can understand."

"For example?" he said, pinning me down.

"The Beatles, Joni Mitchell, Joan Armatrading, Tanita Tikaram, Suzanne Vega, Leonard Cohen, Simon and Garfunkel, Santana?"

"How about dance as well," he said, spinning playfully on the chair and clicking his fingers. I hesitated and told him I'd think about it. Dance, the body, language, music – I felt you knew about this kind of communication, but it would take hours.

"Coffee – how do you like it?"

"Dark – one sugar, not too much milk."

We sat silently, as the sun streamed through the glass. A laser beam, it struck many colours onto the mirror of the ceiling and the smooth surface of the walls; it divided things into many shades. I finished my coffee; so did he. Now Carlos was chasing paper. Fluttering in the whirlwind, the airborne pages danced in circles; they were arrows, paper kites, birds. They were planes about to take off.

I joined in the game, gathering the pages. He closed the window. We were scrambling on the floor now, fighting, competing with each other to grasp the last few pages. Our heads came close. Suddenly, our eyes met. His hands had a roughness. He had a single diamond earring. I found him attractive; he was youthful, lean and energetic. When he stood up, he was about five foot nine. Our eyes met again, this time at a distance.

I thanked him for his suggestions, left him standing

motionless under the whirr of the paddle-blades of a solitary fan. He seemed to be recalling something briefly. I glimpsed him through the glass panel. He made a quick movement with his index finger, and dived towards his desk. He got a pen, scribbled a note on a violet post-it. And then, he was the demi-god again; almost expressionless. Someone else entered. I nearly bumped into them.

"Sorry," we said.

"He's alright," Phil said later. "But be wary, don't cross him – he's a bit of a snake in the grass."

I'd been teaching there several months to help Carlos out. A teacher had bunked off to Liverpool.

"There are reasons why I didn't make bids for all the contracts," he said confidentially, "but you can do this one, if you like."

My boss was a woman in her early fifties. She'd worked in animation in her early days, and was artistic. Then she'd worked as an Education Officer for the Prison Service.

I liked the room I'd be teaching in. It had modern pictures on the walls, and floor to ceiling windows. If it wasn't for the whiteboard, modern desks and swivel chairs, it resembled an art gallery. The light splashed in and I felt happy.

"I'll have to go through the motions of advertising, and the final decision will be with the Chief Executive, but we'd like you to apply," she said.

She showed me the job spec. I recognised myself in 'The Person' outline: 'Capable, innovative, versatile, and interested in curriculum development, empathy for people from different backgrounds and cultures, a dynamic team player.' Yeah, that is me, I thought. It was as if she'd written it for me; I was cut out for it. It was strange applying for the job I'd done for almost a year. Elaine and the Director asked me a few random questions, whilst the other candidates sat nervously on a line of chairs in the corridor.

Elaine looked glamorous for an older woman. I looked down at her shoes. The backs jutted beyond the backs of her ankles. They were roughly two sizes too big. Her eyes followed mine. I think she'd seen that I'd noticed, and then carried on. It was only a year later I'd discover the reason. We had a lot in common. (When I handed my notice into my previous employers, they tried to retain me.)

"You should have talked to me first," Carlos said dejectedly.

"I would have done, but I didn't know how you'd react," I said.

He looked fed up. I was looking after myself, and my risk-taking days would be over.

V

"Hey, Sue," he said, climbing the steps to the front door, "you haven't changed a bit; you look good, mmm, good."

(He looked similar to the man I knew before, except for a slight widening round the waist.)

The flat was the one I nearly bought, in Temple Gate. He grappled with the keys, and as we walked in, he guided me, opening doors, his hand touching my back.

"Well, is it okay?" he asked.

It was better than the High Meadows flat, but in the height of summer it would be like a greenhouse: the rear faced due south, and there was a large glass window. He knew what I was thinking.

"You'll need some blinds for privacy," he said. "It could get quite hot in here."

(Of course, I knew what he meant.)

He still had the same honey-chocolate eyes that I remembered. He was closer now, and I could see the fine fishtails round his eyes that reminded me of my father when he smiled. V's eyebrows were still jet black, and his hair dark. I wanted to touch it, ruffle it through my fingers.

"Hey, Oz," he said, "you know I'm going to have you again."

I turned my back, went to put the kettle on. He came behind me. I could feel his torso and hips against me, hard. He knew the right approach. I dropped the spoon. He picked it up. We kissed a deep French kiss. The magic was still there. There was something in his eyes that always conquered me, and I wanted him. But I wasn't going to say.

The following weekend, he made himself scarce. I was lying on the floor pulling on some white jeans.

"Hi," he said. "Miss you!" (He made an impromptu appearance.)

He jangled his keys. "Want to come for a ride?" A childlike expression flew across his features; he liked the thrill, the speed.

"I'm going shopping."

"I'll take you there and back."

"Really!"

He was rakish, but honest about his feelings.

"May have to go soon."

The shadow of a smile passed fleetingly over his mouth, like the sun fading behind a cloud. Then, the mobile rang; the ringtone was INXS. He stepped over the door ledge, stood on the gravel, and kicked stones as he was talking. His voice was hurried, relaxed. Man talk. The factory, garments, rentals, hired vans, his best friend, 'M'.

"Gotta go now, Sue!" he said. "Give you one hundred and fifty off for a blow job!"

Then he kissed me. Maybe it was the way I curled my lip, and frowned. He apologised immediately, with the look of a schoolboy newly reprimanded. And then the look, under the heavy fringe.

"Your ass in those jeans!" he said. "Want you, mmm, real bad!" He patted me on the cheek enough to sting, winked at me, and left.

"Kneel," he'd say. I could hear his voice in the High Meadows flat. See his eyes, shining with ardour, pupils black orbs.

"Open your legs," he whispered.

Then I held his head in my hands, kissing his hair, caressing his earlobes, stroking the skin on his neck as his tongue swooped down, pleasuring me. A secret dusky rose flowered; my body twitched involuntarily, like a bird with broken wings dying in a shady forest. He was deep in my throat, and now between my breasts. Then we were coming together; intimacy, closeness, a landscape without a map.

I was standing on the bridge that led to the summer school, by the river. A group of students were around me, smoking cigarettes. One was from Spain. We got on well. I guess he was the best of the bunch. He'd just cracked a joke; we were laughing together. Then, on the grassy raised bank in the distance, I saw him. It was the biker. I couldn't be sure, but I thought I'd seen him in my rear view mirror on the way to work. He was clearly not a student; he hadn't a pass. He stood quite still, staring blatantly in my direction. When I left the campus, he picked up my tail as I drove back. As soon as I got to the roundabout, he accelerated and sped off in front of me. It was only when he followed me again, a sharp arrow cutting through the dark, that I felt concerned, but I kept it to myself. I'd vary my route.

V appeared unannounced that very weekend.

"She's away," he said, following me into my room, his navy jacket slung casually over his shoulder, then in a heap on the bed. He kissed me, holding the sides of my face in his hands; he stroked my hair.

"Where in the world have you been all this time," he breathed. Then he pulled away and I began to talk. He had a way of silencing me; he started to unzip my dress, kissing the nape of my neck, softly at first, and now his mouth was circling the dark purple nipple of my breast, until it was swollen.

"Not yet."

He backed off.

"Enjoying yourself with your handsome students these days?"

(There was fire in his eyes, but he wasn't angry.)

"What do you mean?"

"You seem to spend a lot of your break times with your students!"

"How the hell do you know?"

"I have my sources."

"You've had me followed!" I exclaimed.

(He started to laugh. This was the haha moment.)

"Yeah, I knew it would turn you on, so you'd better behave or else!"

"What do you mean?"

"I know something you'll like," he said. "I'm coming back this evening. Think about it, Sue. I'll be here at nine!"

And then he kissed me again, this time with restraint.

Later, he phoned me, at intervals. He phoned me at two. The men would be round in half an hour to fix some blinds. He phoned me at four. Had they left yet? Were the blinds okay? He phoned me at five; he was worried about a deal — what did I think? He phoned me at five-fifty; he just clinched it. It was worth thousands! He phoned me at six-thirty; he'd be round sooner than nine. He phoned me again, at seven. What was I doing now? I told him I was just out of the shower. He kept on talking as he was driving.

The beads of water were trickling down my body like a slow tap, marking the seconds, like the last drops of the shower head. And then I looked, and he was there again in soft focus. He'd come quietly through the back door.

The best advice I've had about sex was from a man in St Albans. He'd been a military man, and an eminent surgeon. Now he was semi-retired; an osteopath.

I'd picked up a parcel on the office floor, a telephone in one hand; I failed to use my muscles properly and hurt my back. I got a lift to the surgery. The doctor took an x-ray, and when the pictures came back, he gave me the verdict: it was a slipped disc. I'd be laid up for weeks on end. No chance, I thought. I wasn't going to follow his advice, and lie on a stiff mattress, missing the action at the office. I'd be miserable and bored out of my skull with that so I sought a second opinion.

"Come in!" he sang. His voice competed with the chime of the grandfather clock. It was six. I could hardly walk in; his receptionist helped me.

"Strip down to your underwear. Don't worry, I can't see you!" he said. He was completely blind; he did everything with his other senses.

"Take off your bra!" he said. "And cover your toys, so I don't play with them!"

He made me laugh. "Now this may hurt," he added. He leaned into me with his full body weight. I could smell the woody, masculine aroma of sandalwood. Nothing happened. Then he put me in a stirrup contraption, and suspended me from the ceiling. And then he put me into a machine that rotated me with a 180° turn. It made me think of astronauts, or some kinky kind of torture chamber, but his manner was exemplary.

The third time I visited, he leaned into me again, all his body weight concentrated in the hands that manipulated my back. "Ouch!" I cried. Something had snapped back into line – I heard it.

"I want you to do some crouching exercises as part of the physiotherapy," he recommended. He asked me to have a try there and then.

"Crouch right down, that's right, so your bottom nearly touches the floor. Good. How does that feel, hmm? Excellent! I tell you what, are you married? Mm. I see. It's a jolly good position for having sex. I strongly suggest you try it!"

I couldn't take offence. He made me laugh, and I knew he spoke from experience. He had lost his sight. But it was as if his other senses were heightened because of that. I'd seen it before, with the blind piano tuner. His hearing was acute, his sense of touch super sensitive.

From touch alone, he could describe my body type. "You're small to medium build," he said, "like an hourglass with a super waist. Maybe a little bit of a pear, but not much!"

I wondered where this was leading. "One leg's significantly longer than the other. Did you have a built-up shoe as a child? No? Well, it must have been borderline. Ask your mother. Your body's at a slight tilt because of that. Like a ship! Oh? You know what I'm talking about, then? You've been sailing! There's a slight pitch and yaw as you walk about. Damned attractive, though! I'd whistle, if I were twenty years younger!"

I was astounded, and I followed his instructions to the letter.

The Enemy I loved

It was in October, just before the betrothal. These days, he's like my favourite impossible child. Petulant, unpredictable, troubled. Yet, I'm not his mother. Why do I need him? I need to be wanted. I support him. I am the strong one.

We went to a party. He drank too much wine. He did his party gig; the man from Peckham could have won an Oscar, people laughed! Then he sat on the table; it shattered, and he looked like a bird in a nest of glass.

"I'll take you to A and E," I said, matter-of-factly.

I drove him there and we stayed all night. The nurse came: a tetanus injection was what was needed, in his rear – it wouldn't hurt – and stitches. I knew about the OCD. Maybe I'd suffer later for this. But he was charm itself; he loved the attention, and was glad he had gone.

When he came from the check-up a week or so later, he showed me the badge. 'I have been good for the nurse' it read, with a picture of a frog – he'd had the sutures out.

"There's something I've got to tell you," he said one day. His face looked pensive. I detected a tightening in his voice. He looked me straight in the eye, his body almost motionless.

"What?" I said.

"I'm in trouble with the law, for a crime I never committed. They're after me! Those guys in Nottingham started it. Get D H, they've got nothing better to do, bastards! Fucking on my back – those pigs in their Noddy cars. If I still had my Ferrari, they wouldn't stand a chance! Thick as shit they are!"

"What are you supposed to have done?" I asked. I thought maybe he had borrowed a car, driven when banned at the very worst.

"Vandalism. I don't remember anything, so I got no alibi. It may go to court."

"But for vandalism, you'd just get a fine, surely?"

"It's more than that."

He looked strained now.

"I think they're accusing me of criminal damage!"

He kept his feelings under wraps. I respected him for that. I speculated he was exercising great control under duress. How noble, I thought. He looked nervous now. And for the first time I noticed the nervous tick, the slight twitch of a shoulder. He was looking at me steadily now, with a fixed, enquiring gaze.

"Never mind," I said. I resolved to get him through it, whatever it was – the wedding was a week away.

"Will you come with me to the solicitor's?" he said.

"Of course, I'll take time off work."

Doyle's barrister was how I imagined: corpulent, self-satisfied, pompous, but incisive and almost kind.

"We're getting married," Doyle said.

"Oh?" said the fat man.

He swung round, and his body seemed to expand; he looked taller and his shoulders seemed to broaden. He stood between me and his client.

"I think it's only right your lady wife to be sees your criminal record."

Doyle appeared to be smaller, his face immobile.

"Yes," he said, under his breath. "All right!"

The printout came winging down onto the table. I felt faint. What could I do? I wanted to be bigger than myself, give him a second chance. Maybe it was pure conceit; I can understand if that's what you think.

I decided to get a man's angle on it, so I asked a close colleague,

115

one with teenage sons; he might throw some light on it.

"It's up to you," Razak said. "But I'd give it more time, if I were you."

"But he needs help!"

My friend looked puzzled.

"He might never change."

"I'm going to take the chance that he will."

"Has he been married before?"

"Yes. He lost his first son. His other son is dying."

"That would make anyone break!"

"That's what I thought."

"Do whatever you want to do; it's your life, Sue."

It was my life. And I wanted to do something fantastic, something inspirational. I believed I could. The wedding came. He didn't want any of my friends there, so we kept it simple. His Irish friends were our witnesses.

The registrar had a sense of humour. He asked, "If you could marry a rock star or a film star instead of her, who would it be?"

"Elizabeth Taylor."

"And what about the lady?"

I thought of a dark stranger, in a video, crooning on the sands; he was wild and windswept, passionate, the stormy sea in the background.

"Bryan Ferry?"

It was just a laugh, and then we said our vows.

A Secret of the Heart

Razak and I liked each other, there was mutual respect. Ko was less spontaneous, but he had a sense of humour, and was wise.

We were talking about how teaching was romanticised in the movies. *Dead Poets' Society*, *To Sir with Love*, *Fame*, and *Educating Rita* – we talked about them all.

Razak Ahmed wanted to be Sidney Poitier.

"What about *The Witches of Eastwick*?"

"I'd be Susan Sarandon!"

(Ko walks off; for him reality is better than dreams – he teaches Mathematics.)

What actor would play you?

"What are you thinking about?" Razak rummages through neatly folded greaseproof paper to reveal freshly baked, mouth-watering samosas, and extends his hand.

"Nothing."

"Did you ever have a favourite teacher?"

I bite into the samosa and pause.

"Yes, but he was more to me than that."

Razak busies himself with his lunch, which Tamsin has lovingly prepared. We sit side by side, our movements mirroring each other. Not a word is exchanged, but the silence is comfortable.

Danger

The warning sign came two weeks after the wedding. What had I done wrong? Nothing – as far as I could tell. He head butted me when he got drunk. He was laughing when he did it. He denied all knowledge in the morning, but he was worried when I left for work. The makeup nearly covered the bruising over the bridge of my nose, but not the swelling. Fortunately it wasn't broken even though it hurt.

I left for work early. Arrived just after eight-fifteen and scurried past the cleaners, saying hello on the hoof. I sat in the gallery room, at my desk, and cradled my head in my hands, thinking. I was hoping nobody would see, when Raz came in.

"What have you done?"

"I don't want the students to know he got drunk."

I told him I was afraid of going home.

"Don't!" he said.

"I think I'll stay in a cheap motel; I don't want to put on anybody."

"What about clothes?"

"Eight for the top, ten for the bottom."

"My wife's the same size as you."

I would borrow Tamsin's clothes, we decided. He brought me a coffee.

"Are you going to tell the police?"

"I'm too scared!"

(I was like a rabbit, caught in car headlights. I remember going back.)

"Where have you been?" Doyle asked.

"I stayed with a female friend."

He never asked. I felt the honeymoon had started all over again.

"I need a bolthole," I told Elaine a few weeks later. "I'm reserving a room at the hostel on Spinney Road."

I'd asked the decorator how I could change him.

"Change his environment, take him somewhere better."

I thought that sounded logical. It didn't pan out exactly as I had planned. That was the flat he followed me to, and he liked it. For a while Doyle seemed content.

"Don't touch my things ever again!" he shouted one morning.

My crime? I'd moved a pen. (Anyone who knows me will tell you I collect them.)

"Sorry," I said.

He said nothing, so I left silently for work. I was worried about going home again, so I braced myself as I opened the door.

"There's a new regime in here," he announced. "I'm drinking my beer in the bedroom from now on!"

"Okay. What time do you want dinner?"

"I don't want to eat till ten!"

I was hungry; I'd just grabbed a sandwich at my desk. I was only allowed to be hungry when he was, I ate when he ate.

"Don't disturb me!"

I could hear him punching the walls in the bedroom. He seemed to be rehearsing a kind of dialogue; I caught the word 'bitch'. That referred to me, I thought. I wanted to leave in an instant, but decided I'd front it out. I read the paper. There was a crime in the middle pages, but I skipped those topics – they were too close. I had to cook for him; we were married. I'm old-fashioned, I suppose. I don't mind if you think I was foolish. I do now.

"What's for dinner?" he demanded.

He seemed to tower over me although he was just five foot nine.

"Spaghetti."

"How much longer?"

"Five minutes and I'll dish up."

"What's the matter with you, bitch?" he cried. "Looking at me like that!"

He went for my face, but I covered it with my arm, which he punched. He tried to follow me as I made my escape, but I got there first. I resolved to tell probation I wanted him to sober up; they could put that on the licence.

"We can't do that. Do you want to press charges?" said Solomon, taking out an *aide memoire*.

"It's only bruised."

"Well, we're going to recall him."

"Please don't."

No choice. An arrest. Safety. But trouble? Yes, trouble later, perhaps.

One day, when he was away, I went to the church. But there was no way out. I had to ask Elaine.

"Many people think the function of jails is rehabilitation," she said, "but it isn't. They're there to protect the public."

I still wanted to work my miracle.

"How can I change him? He's so angry, so bitter!"

"Forgive me for saying this, Sue, but it's difficult to change what people believe."

"I want to try."

I saw his situation through my own experiences: my mother had started to drink when my father died – it was grief. But later I discovered he'd always hit the bottle, even before the bereavements. I'd wanted to rescue Angela; I'd wanted to save him. I was rescuing the mother who was distant, the brother who was quick to anger. They were never as close to me as I'd hoped. But they were all I knew; I married them. It was uncanny. I went to see an analyst, the one who had taught me at his house.

"Your drivers are 'Please People' and 'Be Strong'," he told me. "But it's okay to ask for help. You can't do it all on your own!"

"What could I be doing to trigger this behaviour, John?"

He listened to the history, the *follies à deux* between Helen and Doyle, before.

"I don't think it's you," he advised, "but whatever you do, don't try to persuade him or manipulate him. It could be a personality disorder. If so, he would need many sessions; it could take years."

I asked him a small favour.

"He's got to make the appointment himself. He's got to make the commitment to do it himself!"

When Doyle was in prison, he promised he'd accept assistance. But his first request upon his release was beer, again. It was getting worse. I didn't like it if I got home first; it would be harder to leave if he blocked my way.

A second meeting with Doyle's solicitor ensued. A problem had emerged. There was video evidence and eyewitnesses. Prison loomed large, and the charges were greater than criminal damage. He might get three years.

Now I knew he had lied, minimised what he had done. I felt trapped. He was a powder keg waiting to explode, and he took it out on me. My friend found me a flat, but he tracked me down. He begged forgiveness. It would be different from now on, he declared, staring at the ground. I told him where I lived, and took him back.

We had Christmas. I made it special. The day of the court case came, and the judge spoke:

"I've no doubt there's been a sea change in your life. And you have married a good woman. No doubt she will be a good influence on you. But it is the duty of this court to protect the public."

Within seconds, the female security guards grabbed his arms. He mouthed, "I love you," and disappeared down the steps.

Déjà Vu

It was a lonely drive from Lincoln. I felt drained. But things would be different when he came out. I resolved to absorb myself in work. And I could phone my stepson and his ex-wife. We'd built some bridges together.

It was a sunny spring day when I took the car along a familiar route: to Greatham via Tilton-on-the-Hill. I can still see Greta and me speeding along the undulating road, the kind of roller-coaster ride which puts your heart in your mouth. We were on that very road the day the degree results came. We rode along chatting and laughing all the way. I had butterflies in my stomach. Then I thought of years before, the summers when Colin and I had gone rambling, and had a ploughman's at the pub. A journalist, he knew his geography, and one day we'd stopped short of the prison.

"What's along that road?" I'd asked.

"I think it's a prison, nothing very interesting."

(Now my mind was a palimpsest making alterations. I was writing over the happy times. Suddenly, I felt sad. The memories were changing.)

The setting of the jail was idyllic. A warm glow rippled over the rolling Rutland countryside. I could see the farm in the distance, and the patchwork of wheat and fallow, verdant grass and bright yellow rape seed. As the car climbed to the top of the hill, I saw the walls, the barbed wire, official signs, and security cameras. It didn't seem to belong there.

Prisons are difficult places to enter if you are a visitor. You wait. You get past the dog. Then, they frisk you. (Sometimes women guards linger a little too long.) Finally, you can proceed. You feel like a criminal.

This prison was kinder than the one where there'd been a fire and riots that made the headlines. No screens. You could talk at the table. No touching allowed though. Half an hour; very quickly you become strangers. The last time, I thought he was getting thinner. He asked about Si.

"He rings me once or twice a week," I said, "when his mother's asleep."

"What do you talk about?"

"You, driving, cars, mostly."

"He fancies you," he said. "I wouldn't stand a chance if he were well again."

"Don't be daft, he's my stepson!" (Between us our ages spanned three decades.)

"He said you were beautiful."

I glanced at the man I'd married. Out of an admixture of compassion and affection, I wanted to do my best. And there was always the passion, the sexual attraction, so comforting, yet so dangerous. I missed those nights. "We'll go and see them when you come out," I promised.

One and a half years passed. Doyle got his parole. He was home. I fed him up with roast pork dinners, his favourite. He gained weight. He was still washing money, but not notes, just coins. He wouldn't leave the flat without checking lists. He gambled, and he was drinking, heavily. I endured the situation as best I could. We hired a car to Glasgow. He wanted to drive; the ban had been lifted. He'd mislaid the paper part, so I did.

It was nearly Christmas; I think there was snow, a kind of blizzard. Progress was slow. He wanted me to drive faster but I was doing a hundred as it was. I suffer from night blindness. I felt afraid. As we approached Glasgow, he wanted beer. That was all he seemed to think about, and it was getting worse.

The house was illuminated, stood high on a hill. I could

see the outline of a sylph-like woman, silhouetted against the wall, standing on the doorstep. Doyle bolted towards her, and they exchanged a few brief words. Maybe that's her, I thought. I gathered my things and followed. The kitchen door was slightly ajar. Doyle entered first. "Whatever happened to you?" he asked abruptly.

"I'm an old lady now," came the soft, quavering voice. It was her – it was Helen. The woman standing on the doorstep had been my stepson's girlfriend.

"Hello, Helen," I said.

"Hello. Do you want a glass of orange juice?"

She was surprised he'd remarried. Her eyes looked glazed; she seemed to forget my presence as she unscrewed the vodka bottle and splashed in some ice.

"Do you want some vodka and orange?"

"No thanks," I said. I needed all my faculties.

We went into the lounge together.

"Where's Si?" I asked.

"He's upstairs. Go and see him if you want."

"It's okay," I said, "he'll probably want time with his father first."

Doyle went up, carrying beer and Sterling cigarettes. He came down again.

"He's sleeping now," he said, "but he'd like to meet you later."

The old charm had come back, like the flick of a light switch. Helen was knitting a cable-knit pullover. I thought how worn she looked. "Ten more minutes," she said, entering the kitchen. They exchanged a glance, Doyle leaning forward, Helen peering through the fog at his lived-in swarthy face. I know it must have been difficult; his absence, and her loneliness.

I felt Doyle's hand touch my thigh. He was caressing my breasts as soon as her back was turned. I think, perhaps, in the periphery of her vision, she caught a glimpse by mistake. After dinner, Doyle ascended the stairs.

"You wouldn't believe what Doyle was like when I was married to him...He broke my jaw." I tried not to stare, but I was shaking now. I went to the refrigerator and poured myself a drink. "We'll have a talk sometime, when he's not around."

I didn't like this sudden wedge, this secrecy, this triangle. She reminded me of someone, but I resented her, only a little. A few weeks passed, and then the phone call came.

"You've got to come this evening." Helen's voice cracked.

We had to take a taxi. Probation wouldn't allow it any other way; they feared for my safety. We could report to the police as soon as we arrived. As the taxi approached Glasgow we had to take a detour. "For fuck's sake, find me an off-licence willyer!" When he lost his temper it broke the spell. He didn't sound the same. It was as if a shadow was cast over his features; he seemed to become darker.

"Hello," I said to Helen, looking at the empty bed. "Where's Si?"

"He's there," she said.

There was the smell of sick and urine. His slight frame was swallowed up in the clammy bedclothes. "Where's my boy?" Doyle said, as he tugged at another ring pull on the next can.

"Here," Helen replied. The father sat with a beer can in one hand, and stroked his son's brow with the other. Helen was a good listener; she selected her words carefully. She poured herself another drink. Sometimes, I thought I saw fear in her eyes. She clung to the memory of Doyle, as if he were a habit she could not break.

I recall a later visit, when Simon was sat up in bed, his head resting on the velour headboard, propped up with numerous pillows. He was keen to have an audience with myself and his father. A friend arrived. It was all man talk: racing, something about V8 engines, I can't remember. Talked about the Ferraris

Doyle owned when he was younger. So that was true, and the stuff about Doyle's father. It was deep in winter. Si wanted to see in the New Year; that would make him happy. He seemed to rally, he was in good spirits.

"Darling," I said, "would it be tactless to buy a get well card, just in case we have to go back?"

(Probation was asking how much longer.)

"No," he said, "but don't touch your hair after the door handles, and wash your hands. Kick the door open if it's shut when you return."

"Okay."

"Be strong, Sue," Simon said. He paused, searching his father's face and added, "Be kind to her, Dad."

We said 'goodbye' again, and left.

Doyle and I were in the hotel room, to avoid the feeling of *ménage à trois*, or so I thought. He had been taking an early evening nap, when I came from the bathroom, newly showered and dried. "You in white drives me crazy!" he said. I liked it when he looked, really looked. We'd told Helen we were going back, I thought. But he won; cornered me up against a wall, lifted me onto a chest of drawers, threw me on the floor. Then, into bed. I thought I'd lost all feeling in my legs.

"We're tired," he said apologetically. "We were up all night!" I saw the look on her face; she was trying to avert her eyes. He wanted her to know. When we were on our own, he took me in his arms, kissed me ever so softly on the cheek and said, "I wanted to get rougher with you, I know you like that." And then he smiled that devastating smile. The eyes betrayed the meaning all too well.

Si got his wish. We had Christmas together, and he saw in the New Year. I'd bought him some books, but the print was too small, so Helen read them. But he did watch *Finding Nemo*.

I tried to give Helen a rest. He'd insisted on coming home, but when he wasn't sleeping we took turns with the sick bowl.

126

Then back to the ward; he spent his last days there. Doyle was recalled back to jail just before Simon died. We didn't share the final moments.

"I want to remember him as he was!" Doyle said.

But Helen commented, "He never saw any of us for thirty years!"

I wondered if I'd done the right thing, digging up the past, making connections. It seemed as if Helen was under the old spell again; maybe she expected he would change.

"Doyle," she said on the phone, "let's have *A Whiter Shade of Pale* at the funeral, the song we had on our wedding day." The Queen of the Mods was back. She had married the solicitor who had conducted her divorce. He had helped her when Doyle was nowhere to be found. Later, they divorced as well. Her stepsons attended Si's funeral; Doyle, under a police escort.

Helen's new man friend was at the farewell, a psychotherapist. Helen told Doyle they were splitting up. Who knows the mystery of love between a man and a woman? Maybe only them. Can love and fear coexist, side by side? I thought not. I decided it was deeper than that. "Whatever you do, get a divorce," she advised, "before it's too late."

They say: "Don't worry."

"Act as if you don't care."

On the way back, on the train from Glasgow to Reddington, I milled over her words, and questioned her motives.

Quite a lot happened when he came back. I started telling myself not to do things. When I sat down, I didn't walk around at any point, sometimes for hours, always sat in exactly the same spot, not far from the exit. When I cooked, I cooked simple dishes – the less preparation, the less clattering of pans. (I moved the Sabatier knives to the Volkswagen, except on Sundays. In Korea, shamans can dance on knives and don't get hurt. I wouldn't dare try myself.) I didn't watch Jon Snow, my favourite broadcaster, because it annoyed him. He played what music he liked, loud. When I left one day, in a hurry, I phoned Elaine from my bolthole.

"I could use some company," I said.

"Yeah, me too!"

He'd thrown her out. She often had to stay at her daughter's. The flat was above a flower shop, and had a huge, open plan lounge. The colour scheme was contemporary, in pink and white and black. Every room had a mirror, and in the dining area were Christmas tree lights, although it wasn't that time of year. In the sitting area, the windows looked out onto people in the street below.

We went into Elaine's bedroom. It had yellow and olive green walls. On one wall was an antique picture in reds, greens and blues. It featured a roving knight in armour, and a damsel with Titian hair, in a red velvet dress with a ruffle at the neck. It was called *The Betrothal*. I love that word! On the door of her room was a picture of Jesus, with the words, 'I am the light of the world.'

The fragrance of lilies pervaded the room: pervaded the linen French pillowcases and bed sheets, pervaded the lace and cotton of her nightgown, which was hung from a picture rail near the window, and was trembling like a leaf in the wind. The room was as light and sweet as a garden in springtime. There was just enough space for an old French bateau bed. The cherry wood had a patina like a mirror. The antique desk was cluttered and colourful. It had a display of scented candles, and jewellery of natural polished stones. There was a single ornamental dagger, and a case with the bones of a crocodile. Raz at work had given it to her.

"Why does she want it?" he said.

"It's probably for her spells!"

Now, as I looked at the desk, something was staring back at me: the eyes of a stuffed bird. I shifted back. "We rescued the bird from a road accident. After it died, we kept it," she said. I remember seeing those things in museums on school trips as a child. My father didn't like them either. Once something was dead it was dead, and that was it. He had a particular dislike of caged birds like the ones my aunt in Purley kept.

"They're unhygienic!"

"They're meant to fly!"

As I write, I think of Maya Angelou, and a woman called Diana; my father was indeed a visionary and wise. A class I taught the other day taught me about Korean culture. According to Korean folklore, men are wolves. But women can transform themselves. Maybe it comes from Shamanism or Totemism, I'm not sure. Anyway, women are sometimes rabbits, sometimes foxes, sometimes bears. A pretty, innocent woman is a rabbit; a cunning, double-crossing seductress is a fox. A woman who cares for others more than she does herself is a bear. I tell them that in Britain, we often think of women as being like birds.

When these words come, here you are again. I can see you, in one of your skittish moods. You're personalising your lecture, showing me that you're a man. I'm sitting further away than usual, about two seats from the wall, on your right, several rows back. It is difficult, trying not to show how I feel, trying to quell the almost inexpressible emotions that assail my heart. But this is how to know. Do you look for me in my usual space, notice my absence? I am watching you! There's a carefree smile on your face, and your green eyes sparkle.

"I like bird watching," you say. I can see the words leap out from a page, framed by an arrowed arch and a dark flash. (You know I'm holding my breath now.) "...of the feathered variety."

I used to throw javelin for school on Sports Day. I was strong. I was a female warrior. And your aim was straight. It hit home.

If I were a bird, what kind of bird would I be? What do you think? I want to know.

Birds of a Feather

"Did you see Elaine, snogging in the car park?" Raz said.

"No," I replied.

"He didn't look like her type at all!"

"What do you mean," I said, "not professional?"

"No, not at all!" he said.

"Maybe she likes a bit of rough!" I quipped.

"I couldn't believe it!" he said. "They both looked rather dishevelled."

"The just-out-of-bed look?" He nodded. "I won't interfere with her life," I said, "but what if her husband finds out?"

He was taking a last puff on a Marlboro cigarette, and, putting it tidily into the butt bin, said, "No doubt she'll tell us when it all goes wrong." Then we went back to our classes.

The court case came. I never wanted it, but the CPS insisted on prosecuting, so I had to appear in court. They said I'd have screens to make it easier, but the day came, and they'd forgotten. The Witness Protection Service consisted of a frail, elderly woman; a kind layperson. My lawyer was just out of law school. Doyle was well rehearsed and had the best reptilian lawyer in town, all for free. We lost; police mislaid some papers. I had a two-hour wait. Doyle was eloquent, and cracked jokes to make light of it. "It was a Churchillian wave that went wrong," he opined.

I think there should be an intelligence test for jurors. I marched out in disgust – I could tell, before the result, they would release him in days. I didn't want to leave my home, in my name only, and quit my job. I didn't want to part with things of sentimental value: my childhood photos, my mementos, my books, my certificates, my diaries. I left in my clothes, having resolved to spend the night at The Comfort Hotel.

"Come round! I'm at my daughter's," Elaine said, on the telephone. (On the table, in the lounge of the Pink Palace, there was a jigsaw of cats in progress.) "What film do you want, Sue?" she asked. I said I didn't mind. We watched *Chocolat*, with Johnny Depp. I like Magic Realism, and all things French. We cosied up like sisters on the sofa. She decanted some Cabernet Sauvignon into Bohemia Crystal wine glasses. "Oh dear," she sighed. "Why is it that I only like bad boys?"

But I could think of one good boy I liked. He seemed untouchable, impossibly unreachable. I was ashamed of my failures. I wanted him to see that I was all woman, strong.

The Past Comes Back

"I want to put some flowers on Simon's grave," Doyle announced, "on Sunday."

"Okay," I replied.

"I know roughly where he was buried, Helen told me," he said.

The funeral had been in Glasgow. But Si had been cremated and the ashes buried in a little churchyard next to Butch, his late brother. I drove Doyle to the village; it was not far from Nottingham. We stopped and parked.

"Is that it?"

"No, it's a small burial ground with headstones, near a field where they keep horses."

The wind was sharp, but the sun came out as we walked along from the church with the daffodils that billowed through the high grass on the burial ground, raised high above the road.

"I don't think it's along here," he said, turning back.

"I've got a feeling it is!" I replied.

He resolved to phone Helen. Into the periphery of our vision, a gentleman appeared with a weathered country face; he looked wise. As we spoke to him, he dismounted. We asked about the grave, and he pointed to where we'd gone. I thanked him. He remounted. He nudged his mare with the stirrups, and saluted us before moving off. Doyle was still questioning whether it was the right place. Then, I realised that the horseman had moved off noiselessly on his black steed. Like a spectre, he had vanished into dust.

"Let's just go a little further," I suggested.

We reached a small graveyard, went through the iron gate. There was a keeper's cottage next to it, and horses in fields of green which rolled forever on, into infinity. I thought Doyle looked attractive in the soft navy cashmere coat I'd bought him at Christmas. His hair was freshly washed, and he wore the riding boots he'd worn for the races. "Si would like this," he said, his strangulated voice choking back the tears. Then Doyle noticed the inscription on Butch's plaque. His stepfather's surname was written in stone. It was a cruel blow. "Someone must have forced him!" (I remember you asking me if one man's name is as good as another's. I've been slow in changing my name back. But my father would have known what I thought in my heart.) Time would pass. "Everything passes," my late mother had said. And I thought that in time, Doyle would recover.

"I'd like to go to Saxelby, where I used to live with Helen, and show you the cottage," he said.

"Okay," I agreed. "I miss rambling, is it good for walks?"

He reminded me of Dad in that way: he talked more when he was moving, in a car or walking. The more he talked, the more I felt I'd understand; I'd learned how to listen. "Let's go down Covert Lane. I want to look at something," he said. The lane was leafy, and at one end was a cricket ground. Three-quarters of the way down was a neo-Georgian house, with a cottage garden to the sides, and trees creating shadows at the back. It was isolated. At the end of the road was an unkempt footpath. You could see Coppingstone in the distance on a clear day. All in all, it was a lovers' lane.

He wanted to show me where he'd played cricket. I could imagine him in the whites, the Ilie Năstase of cricket; brilliant and temperamental, the idol of middle-class lady spectators. He often got trapped in the changing cubicles because he couldn't unlock the doors with his bare hands, but the team tolerated his idiosyncrasies. It was 'scare' I decided. As we approached the white cottage, he paused.

"That's where I lived with Clarissa," he said.

"How did you get to know her?"

(He was a vague historian.)

"I used to walk this way sometimes."

"Was she married?"

(My intuition told me she had been, before she'd met my husband.)

"Yes, but I was nothing to do with the break-up!"

"How long were you together?"

He never answered. I decided not to pursue it, or else he'd explode.

"She was a horsy type. She was an accountant."

As we approached the village of Saxelby, he talked about how they'd bought the cottage. He believed that disabilities were contagious. He'd been livid at Helen for buying it from a disabled person. Privately, I thought how illogical that idea was. There would be a higher incidence of disabilities amongst the medical profession if that were the case; it was highly improbable. "They've painted it yellow."

I stole my first glimpse of the cottage. It was bathed in sunlight. There was a balcony off the master bedroom. I imagined dinners by candlelight in summer – him and her.

"What was it like inside?"

"It had a cherry wood floor and staircase – Helen would have nothing but the best!"

Rebecca, a book I'd read years ago. It was a strange premonition, a situation I seemed to know. I always tried to go back, but he made it impossible. We walked hand in hand, by the old telephone box. Three schoolgirls, laughing and fresh-faced, watched as we kissed under the shade of overhanging trees. They were following us. I think they wanted to see what lovers did in spring, wading through the flowers under a canopy of leaves.

When we were nine, my best friend Jan asked if I knew the

facts of life. I remember something of my answer. "Yes, I do," I'd said. "The world is round, although they used to think it was square, and that you could fall over the edge. We are not the only intelligent life in the universe. There may be aliens on another planet, like the moon or Mars, but nobody can prove it!" Jan laughed out loud. She knew the world – 'willy' and 'hole' – and explained the mechanics. Her mum had told her.

"Try, try, and try with your studies, Bach. Romance can wait. *Uch a vee!* You don't understand that men are animals! You are too young to know about such things! Put your education first!"

"I never had your brother till I was forty-two."

"Sure, it's great being single and all. Make them wait!"

"Eurgh!" I said. "If that's what you've got to do to have a baby, I'm not having any!"

"I think you may think about it differently when you're older."

"I wish I'd had my children young!"

"One is enough!"

"Listen, Bach, try with your studies. There's plenty of time for that, see, when you're older. Avril got a degree in French and German – joint honours. Honours, mind!"

Maybe they were curious. We were, when we were young. But Doyle wouldn't make love in the open air, in the woods or the fields. Everywhere was contaminated. It was like being reborn into a world of fear. "Be careful!" he said, as I nearly brushed my hair against the weeping willow. Other people's heads had been there. As we approached the ridgeway, there was a house on a hill. It looked desolate, abandoned. The curtains, scorched and faded by sunlight, were closed. The garden was overgrown.

"Who lives there?"

"Someone does."

*

135

As we left the village, we went past the cottage. "Stop!" he ordered. A middle-aged woman with a Hermès scarf and permed grey-brown hair was walking a Labrador and a Collie. I rolled down the window so he could speak to her. "Remember me?" he said. "The bad boy of the village! Used to live at the cottage." Her lips moved and her face was visibly drained of any colour, but I didn't hear what she said. Her face was still unanimated. He waved as we drove off. She seemed to walk briskly. I didn't see if she waved back.

"Where did you live when you broke up with Helen?"

"Burton Lazaars," he replied, "a house with a swimming pool."

I shivered. That must have been cold, I thought.

"How long did you live there?"

He told me his story, a tale of a mansion with a bell, and a gardener; his parents' house with the plaque on the roof, '1896', where he spent his childhood. His late grandfather was a vet who had employed servants and maids, just as my grandmother had done.

The man I had married was drinking too much. Just as his grandfather did; it ran in the family. When he finished his rounds, the old boy used to go by pony and trap to his favourite watering holes in town. Gwendolyn knew by the time on the clock exactly where he was, and when Doyle's grandfather keeled over, drunk in the seat, the pony knew the way home.

We stopped at an offie before going back. Then Doyle washed the cans under the hot tap before opening them. The alcohol, he claimed, was self-medication. But I dreaded the times he got drunk – too much baggage. He wanted me all to himself, like a possession.

When I was young, I had a recurring dream, a dream that looked like a watercolour painting. I was in Jerusalem. A group of lepers were on the banks of the river. I could see a temple, sun streaming across the mosaic mirror of the dome in the distance. One of the lepers fell into the current. The drowning man flailed his arms, his voice fading as still further the whirlpools took him. I wanted to help him. I was part of a multitude on the opposite bank. They couldn't swim. They might drown. He was contagious. I lifted my head above the crowd and said, "I can't swim well, but I'm going to try."

The gathering of people groaned in disapproval. I dived into the water, and came out a heroine, in robes that dazzled with water-beads, like rainbow sequins. It was peaceful.

The crowd moved on, happy. There had been a miracle. The leper's skin was clear; he would live. Then I caught sight of my own reflection. I knew that I, not he, was the leper.

A local newspaper column informed me recently that Burton Lazaars used to be a leper colony.

The Enigma

"No one is one hundred per cent bad!" I said.

Raz had counselled me to leave. Doyle had rung me at work that day.

"I need two hundred pounds, and if you don't bring it, I'll be waiting for you!"

He was going through an episode again; magical thinking. His jottings were full of numbers, calculations of odds. Messages he'd received from disembodied voices, messages meant for him. Signs on number plates that foretold what would happen.

Mary looked sad.

"It's happened again?"

She and the accountant came home with me.

"I don't want to see your face!"

He was at the top of the stairs. So, I posted the envelope through the letterbox. Maybe you think I was a coward then – others have. The next time, I asked for a police escort. Two tiny women appeared.

"You're even smaller than me," I said. "What if he overpowers you?"

"We're trained in combat. Do you think it's acceptable, him demanding money like that?"

What choice did I have? I thought of the shire horses. Big, strong, beautiful; I could be like one of them. I'd be his workhorse. I could put up with the *Sturm und Drang*. I hoped that he wasn't taking drugs.

"Have you seen the film," Elaine said, "with Russell Crowe?"

"No," I said. (But afterwards I watched it, and I understood.)

"He's a tortured genius."

He hadn't lied about the motor racing. We'd trawled through the microfiches in the library.

His reality was different, that was all. I spoke to his probation officer.

"He needs help."

"He's a long way from being statemented."

"He knows what he's doing!"

I remembered the time I'd told him I loved him, the time he needed to hear it the most. It could break anyone, that kind of tragedy.

"You don't know how evil I am!"

That night, I was wide awake. I watched him in deep slumber. His head was like a stone bust of Stalin, or Lenin, or Mussolini, the features tranquil amidst the chaos, the wreckage.

I'd been reading a book called *Scar Tissue*. It was about dementia. Alcohol pickled the brain, drugs rewired it, and dementia meant you lost connections. I know that from my mother. Maybe it soothed the anguish, if, growing weary, you wanted to forget. It seems the circuit in some people's heads is different from the rest of us.

I'd never asked Helen for help. I felt I couldn't make demands on her; she had enough to cope with. But once, just once, I asked her what she thought.

"Don't even try," she said. "It would be a lifetime's work to understand him."

I reflected on when we first married, and the legal case. His defence was loss of memory. The plaintiff's solicitor asked for medical evidence.

"You just watch," he said. "Those kinds of people think they're brilliant, but I can outsmart them any day!"

A highly qualified psychologist visited him. She asked me to leave the lounge, for privacy. Her test consisted of reading out lists of numbers in sequences, and remembering words. (A high school student could have done it, but the skill was in the final interpretation, I guess.)

I could hear his dulcet tones as he struggled. I was thinking of my dear old dad, and how he was a compulsive list maker. His arteries were clogged, and his brain starved of oxygen.

As the overweight bespectacled spinster blob descended the stairs, a gleeful, mocking smile appeared on Doyle's face.

"Well?"

"It will be okay."

The report came back: there was no apparent loss of memory. Moreover, the psychologist observed that he was of average intelligence.

Summer was beginning to fade.

"Let's go to Reddington Races!" my demon lover said.

He was actually my husband, but that was how I thought of him then. He was the archetypal mid-life crisis, a late teenage rebellion. Maybe I'm being harsh with myself; other professional women had fallen for the charms of his silken voice, and his body warmth.

"What's it like there?" I said.

"You'll love it!" he replied. "The horsy woman, she was like you! She loved it; she loved the colours, the spectacle, and the sound of hooves clamouring for places at the finish, the sweat, the blood, and the craic."

Maybe a distraction would help, I thought. So I put on my camel coat, my brown leather boots, and my trilby hat, which was like my father's. He donned his long, dark green coat and riding boots, and we left.

The theatre brought out the actor, the performer in him. He relished the excitement, the brush with shady characters, and people of almost royal blood.

"How much is it to get in?"

"Oh, we won't bother paying!"

"But there'll be barriers, and a ticket stand!"

He had a touch of mischief in his eyes, and was walking rather more upright than usual. He gave her the killer look.

"Where's the way in?"

His voice was plummy. The woman's eyes surveyed him up and down, with a mixture of enquiry and admiration.

"You're owners?"

"Yes. We had some difficulties with the horseboxes. We're down from Newmarket!"

He didn't seem to have rehearsed it. Maybe it was in the blood, as he'd often boasted. (An ancestor was a celebrated pantomime artist, and this was beginning to resemble one.) He knew I'd appreciate the play on words, the double entendre, and I wanted to laugh.

"People can tell you're high class, though you try to hide it."

How snobbish and flattering that remark was! He had underplayed his perceptiveness, his sharpness, his adaptability, his intelligence, his dishonesty. The Irish called him a 'lovable rogue'. "Sure," Lillian says, "he's a little bit of a weirdo. But all right in small doses." She hands me an ornament of the Virgin Mary. "Pray to the Holy Mary, Mother of God!" I notice she has a gold chain round her neck. It has the Holy Cross and a shamrock. It is 10pm. Her children crowd the kitchen, crowd around her for the first thing they get to eat since coming back from school. Lillian's clothes reek of chip-fat. Their faces gaze upward, in the manner of fledglings in a nest. "Please, Ma," they plead. "Please, Ma." The youngest is angry, pulls on the hem of her skirt and gestures impatiently, like Doyle. Like his child.

"Sure, next time," my single cousin Brian advised me, "I know you like wedding cake, but don't marry them. Play the field!"

The sun shone on the punters, the ticket touts and the riders. The ground was firm, the going, good, according to the race expert in the local newspaper. I put my money to win on a favourite, 'King's Country'. It came in first.

Doyle was elated as well. He'd done the calculations, phoned an Irish tipster that he knew. We went home and ate a big salad; Doyle didn't drink much beer. I knew that look. We went to the bedroom. He forgot about his OCD and kept on his boots. It was like sleeping with Clint Eastwood; he could be mean as well.

Survival

I was working under the assumption that if you do more of the same you get the same result. Doyle was getting hard to handle again. He came back one afternoon, his face like stone. He dived to the sink. Then he was washing his hands, frantically. He made no eye contact. He was like an automaton. I hid in the bedroom to give him space.

When I went to make the coffee, that's when I noticed. There was blood splattered on the carpet, and Doyle had blood on his hands and polo shirt. I paused, and in a low voice I asked, "What have you done?"

"Ah, it's nothing!" he said. "You should have seen them, the Afro-Caribbeans, by the time I'd finished with them!"

There was an almost imperceptible line of sweat on his lip, and his hair was limp with perspiration. His jeans were muddied. It was the first time I'd really noticed his hands. How had I overlooked them, the hands that had caressed and comforted me, and the hands that had delivered blows? The knuckles were completely smashed, the little finger rigid, and hooked.

"I had to settle some scores."

"About what?"

"You don't need to know," he said, his face downcast.

I wondered if there would be a knock at the door. I needed to redirect his energies, occupy his hours whenever possible.

"Shall we go to the races?"

I got the sullen, brooding look.

Then, a few days later, he said he would go. There was an

Irish horse he fancied; he knew the stables, it was a sure thing. In the car park, he indicated the space. I judged the narrow space, parked three spaces away. He was incensed by that.

"That's it! You fucking idiot! I'm off – you're on your own from now on!"

I'd already given him the money. I couldn't face him coming in later, probably drunk. So I begged him.

"It's such a lovely afternoon!" I said, squinting into the overhead sun. It was baking.

"Well, you watch the race outside; I'm going to Ladbrokes!"

My heart sank and began pounding in my chest. It was going to be difficult again, I knew it. If I left the racecourse, he would accuse me of having affairs, meeting lovers. I was faithful. But if I stayed, I'd have to hide what I thought, not seem to monitor or judge. I would never dare complain about anything. He had power. He was drunk again, in a rage, swearing under his breath again.

"Hey up, he's a wrong'un!"

"Come on, darling!"

"I think, maybe, I should go for a walk?"

"Do what you fucking want!"

Then I thought of dinner; it was my duty, however I felt. I followed him meekly indoors, tried to keep out of his way. He was washing more cans. An hour went by, and I was fixed to the spot, drinking coffee at the glass-topped table. He started to mutter under his breath, gave me an ice-cold stare.

Instinctively, I knew it was dangerous. His face was ashen with disproportionate rage. He started to shout. And then the fist came crashing towards my face, which I moved at the last second. The fist smashed the glass into smithereens; into jagged, triangular pieces. The fist was bleeding. I didn't speak. I ran.

He was on a strict curfew now. He'd have to return to the hostel by eleven. He'd said he wanted to disfigure me, like Helen, for what I had done. And that was nothing. I'd have to phone Mina again, ask for her comments.

Returning home never felt the same. He'd eaten both dinners, so I'd gone hungry. There were Stella beer cans strewn across the floor, and a wine bottle, empty. There was no note of apology.

I stood in the wreckage, then started to clear up. I wouldn't phone his sister – she'd think me a fool. And fear freezes the limbs and the voice.

It happened on the way to the bail hostel, the one near town. His fist went through my car windscreen. Staff at the hostel saw it. Doyle still had a curfew. She had been worried about lifting it, but Mina wrote to the Home Secretary; he was given chance after chance.

After New Year's Eve I became withdrawn; we hardly shared anything. I didn't want to be in our bed. I was in your arms. The fantasy felt safe, comforting. You'd probably married a stuffy researcher who wore glasses, a pencil skirt with a crisp white blouse, and Bally shoes. I secretly feared that.

The last thing I recall is the night at the Eco House, in the grounds of a school. We were coming from the dog races, in Wolverhampton. He insisted we turn off there.

"So what do you think I'm going to do now – kill you?" he murmured in an 'I love you' breathy voice.

I shrank into myself, speechless, as his hands moved to grip my throat. Then I found the small voice: "Don't," I said, "I'm your wife!" Seconds later, the car door sprang open. He disappeared into the undergrowth. Minutes passed. I reversed the car, towards the main road. The engine stalled, and he emerged from the bushes. My new passenger wore a crazy fixed stare. My knees were trembling.

"Drive, bitch!" he ordered. A reflux of sick hit the back of my throat. I clung to the slippery wheel. On my lap was my handbag: my life-raft. I was struggling to breathe… And there was a winged creature stirring in my heart.

Watercolours

"Is it going to rain?" Catherine said, a frown across her forehead.

"There may be rain on Saturday," June replied.

She'd listened to the weather forecast. We were going to Geoje Island, on the South Sea, to see the lighthouses and if the weather was fine, to Wado. It was famous for European style gardens.

The journey took four hours. The road snaked round the mountains, which were more angular than those in Wales; it wound down, and further down to the bay, with lobster nets and fishing boats, and fishermen in the jetty. We climbed to the high grassy bank, where a sure-footed goat was grazing. Catherine put her hand across her brow to shield her eyes, June put on a baseball cap, and I wore my sunglasses.

"I want to work in Europe," Catherine said.

She's a nurse, in one of my conversation classes. I imagine her at the hospital beds in cancer wards. I know she's good; she listens well. There's sincerity in her eyes, and steeliness as well. I guess we like people who are most like ourselves.

June is the independent type. She scrambled down the bank onto the granite below, just out of reach of the swirling foam, getting closer, greyer now.

"Is it going to rain?"

No one seemed to know. But the wind was high, and the boat was cancelled.

I wondered if we might see a rainbow. There was a light shower: warm rain. We sheltered under a craggy tree. In the distance were the lighthouses, one more prominent, white against the brooding sky. Startling – you could see it for miles. It beckoned us forward. The other was painted in dark rose, surrounded by water. It was hidden, mysterious. It seemed to whisper across the waves, "Come over, come closer!"

I wondered if a boatman could take us. It was nearer than the island.

"Fishermen won't take us," June said. (I thought we could offer to pay them.)

"It's an old superstition."

"They think that women would spoil the catch!" Catherine said.

"Or something happens to the boat," June added.

"You mean drowning?"

The sun had gone in now.

"Yes," they said.

"The sailors think we're mermaids," I told them.

"Why do you say that?"

"It's a folktale," I said. "A long time ago, when ships were lost, and so were men, they thought that the sound of sirens singing had lured men to their deaths."

I told them tales of Wales, and lifeboats, and of Hans Christian Andersen, and *The Little Mermaid*. (Colin and I had gone to Odense on our honeymoon.)

The mercurial sea goes with my spirit, as do islands and rivers. Take me to where rivers dance with oceans; our identities are fluid. We are countries, territories without borders. Past shipyards, with giant metal claws descending from a shimmering, bejewelled sky, we journeyed forward. Past lighthouses, past the illusive island, which looked like a miniature forest in the sea; it was covered with foliage. We travelled through mountains with windswept, gnarled terraces of pines, and still further, past burial mounds, which sheltered the bodies of the dead like a mother sheltering her young. The Mountain God protected them, while The Bear, in the northern hemisphere, gazed down at them, ever watchful.

We swept through the mountain pass, and through tunnels underground, the lights like those on runways. I thought we were birds, flying through a pink-tinged sky, amethyst near the angular peaks.

"We'll return again," June said, placing her camera into a bag.

We'd visited the museum which housed the works of a famous writer and a book called *Land*.

"What about her life?" I asked. But there are things you can't translate.

Journey Beneath the Stars

"Let sea-discoverers to new worlds have gone,
Let maps to other, worlds on worlds have shown,
Let us possess one world; each hath one, and is one."
— John Donne

A cartographer once drew a map of the world shaped like a heart. How much of earth is truly land – how much to the east, and how much west? Were maps, as they were charted representative of where they sailed? They say Magellan, a great seafarer, discovered the world was shaped like a map. Maybe they knew that one hundred years before him, then remembered again. Maybe there were contenders who got there first.

He never completed his journey, but lit the way for others in his wake. The journey begins in the west, where the sun sets. To the east, the sun rises. We are born a circle; to begin again. How can the world have margins? How can the world have ends?

To the Land of Fire and Snow they sailed. Ships were lost, and so were men. St Elmo's fire lit the passage of the sea for them, and the land breathed bonfires and smoke. They encountered sea wolves, and flying fish, who swam in each other's shadows. There were women who navigated in canoes, holding their children, the beguiling wind blowing soft sleet kisses raining upon their skins. Some say they saw painted giants, long before Darwin.

When they showed them their god, the tattooed savages danced. And some say sailors raped the native women, robbing them of what was theirs. The man that survived was a minion, who understood them, and spoke the same tongue.

The story goes that Magellan was wounded with a bow and arrow and cutlasses, and then a javelin put an end to him.

This much is true: he was brave. Species of birds were named after him, and clouds of stars beyond the Milky Way. Man leaves his trace on earth, sometimes long after he has gone, and the great are always named after *une étoile*.

So, what of the unsung heroes and heroines? What stories would they tell? Who were the wives, the daughters, the guides in the storm? Who sailed with Shakespeare? Whose histories would they know?

Life was an adventure when I was young, just me and Jan in our small world. When you are small, it's easy to look at the sky and wonder about God. I imagined that God might be an astronaut, or a giant bird, like the pictures of cave drawings in history books.

Did you have a name before? I could have known you before I knew The Word, and what it meant. I love you, my conquistador, and was I yours? I try in vain to hide my heart that bears a trace of you, a longing to be close again, that only I can feel, or say about, or show.

I want to know all the names you are. Encounters are always firsts. You and I are seas, communicating with each other, naming and renaming each other, remaking ourselves over and over. Sing with me, let me be your siren. Play me like a harp. I carry the note, the thread, into a tapestry of stars. The meaning of a light here, a shadow there, is in its relationship to others.

An eclipse is when the light goes out on the world. The sun is out there. When we're apart, we stand like stone monoliths; timeless, we make fire. The sea is rushing in now as unconsciousness does. I can see a chord, hear gospel songs and rhythms, as we hoist the sails. The sails are a soft white bird. We are airborne. We are primitive.

Granite and Rainbow

The class of 2010. There have been many classes, but there's always one you remember: the class with Lia, the girl with the laugh like a waterfall, like wind chimes.

How much of themselves do teachers put into their lessons? How many sweet vignettes play out in their classrooms, seeming to fulfil their dreams?

And so Lia and John were like two magnets in a microcosm, about to collide. I imagined them on a first date in a coffee shop, Lia nursing a cup of lemon tea in her little hands, the hands with silver bracelets tinkling. She flutters the long graceful fingers as she talks, the hands with pale ethereal pastel talons, a different colour on every nail. When they caught the light, they looked like beams of sun.

Koreans say that fingernails contain your soul. You shouldn't cut them in public, only in your house. They wrap the clippings in paper or else the spirits can steal their soul away before they are dead.

I imagined my Lia, the girl with the vague look and incisive brain, going for the first time to meet his parents. He'd be bashful and awkward, telling her that dentistry paid well, and that he'd look after her. She'd tell him she wanted three children, two boys and a girl, and she wouldn't mind giving up the flying. His parents would approve.

"Work in pairs," I said.

John was tongue-tied at first, and Lia said, "You're lucky to be working with me!"

John retreated into a world of facts, and criticised the

subjectivity of her thinking. But I know he could tell that she was not stupid, because he was smart. He saw a promising future.

"What are you going to do with the rest of your life?"

He told me he wanted to practise dentistry in Korea, and then build a hospital in Africa. I imagined my Lia there, looking after sick children; one on each arm, one pulling at the waves of unruly hair, pulling at her bracelets as she skipped down the corridors, a fey spirit from another world. And John would organise things, and do the budgeting and the paperwork. He would be the rock my sunbeam girl would rely on.

"I've always wanted to help people," Lia said. "I'd like to go to Africa."

I thought this was their future, but the bubble burst.

You see, she wanted to fly. Would I teach her one to one? She wanted coaching for the interview – what questions would they ask? She had a long lost love, a pilot who worked for Cathay Pacific.

"Of course, I'll help you!" I said.

(I wondered about John; they'd become close.)

"When I went to the hotel he emailed," she confided, "but he's never ask me how it went!"

(The class had a new teacher, and he'd stopped going.)

She was anxious about the interview on Saturday. We sat in a quiet corner in a downstairs coffee shop like two conspirators, composing a CV, rehearsing questions. She turned to me and said, "Suzy, you are so kind and clever. It's as if someone has given me a present, know what I mean? I've met foreigners before. Men, they don't wanna be a friend, know what I mean? And you and my mom told me to be careful of girls. It's true they let me down, they don't wanna help me! They're jealous. You know, because you're experienced. And you have help me more than anyone. You are my English mom. Someone has given me a present. Know what I mean? After I'm with you good feeling keep on. Still feel good when you're not there. Know what I mean? I feel happy after I see you."

It sent a shiver down my spine. A little Indian girl had told me the same thing, more or less. When she was in India, she used to herd buffalo. Some people are unforgettable.

A Song

You knew how to jive; maybe they all do in Australia.

The club was dark. People moved like shades under the strobe lights. Thank you, you took me dancing. You threw me in the air. I was a feather. You caught me. I took a walk round the edge. It was 2pm. I wanted to slip out into the darkness, alone, outside.

"Where are you from?"

"England."

"You have a beautiful face."

I thought of you and the Mersey beat poets. I wish I'd written 'Humdinger' and that you'd follow me to the ends of the earth.

On the way home I strolled by fountains, with the pulse of lights. I thought I could see you on a dance floor. You'd be sensational. I'd wear a red dress, with laces down the back.

Dancing does it for me. You see, I'm highly strung. Your hands were pulling at the laces. They fell to the floor, undone.

"Where did you get to?"

"I thought of something I wanted to write."

"Oh?"

The Swing

When I danced, it reminded me of carefree days, in the garden beneath the elm tree. I was eight or nine then.

"Tick, tick, tock."

It was in the languorous days of summer, on the swing. I could hear the creak of the sturdy rope rubbing against the trunk, feel the wind against the flesh of my thighs as it gathered up my skirt.

The rhythm was a metronome, keeping time on the piano. When I closed my eyes, I was a trapeze artist, treading the wire; sometimes it felt like I was flying.

He was there. Throwing me up, high up, his square hands ready should I fall.

The Dark Lover

I can't remember the year exactly. 1999, at a guess. I was teaching, doing my MA; two things at once. I neglected him – no sex anymore. I wanted to prove myself to those who were absent. I coasted the first year, but now the dissertation loomed, and fears of failure. It became an obsession.

He was working in Eastbourne, I was in Brighton. It was a weekend, or maybe a day off. The world got darker. There was going to be an eclipse.

"Let's go to the beach," he suggested.

The sky deepened to dark blue moiré. The towering waves roared. So high, a wall of water.

"I'm going back!" I said.

I climbed the hill to the flat with the garden of stones and shells, driftwood and sea holly, and hollyhocks against the mossy tumbledown walls, plus the familiar black cat with 'Kater' on his collar; he belonged to a neighbour who loved Latin.

I descended to the basement, put the lights on. I imagined the sea, carrying words like jetsam and flotsam, debris cast off, like lines from a tongue. Sebastian never appeared before dusk these days.

"How was your day? Why so late?"

He did not answer. Jenny said she was Polish, but I still loved him as a friend.

When the eclipse came, I was sitting alone. I thought it may be the end of the world. You were out there, somewhere. I could hear your heart. It was a strong pulse, a rhythm to write by. I paused, and took up my pen. It was eerie, listening to the silence. Where were you now? How could I know? I think I'd know you in the darkness, if you spoke.

"What would be left if ever the world was dark?"

"Listen. And here comes the scream, the primal moment."

"Would I know who I was?"

"There would always be touch."

"What do you feel like, my lover?" I recall your voice, murmuring. "I want your skin."

I remember Hugh; Hugh of hospital radio, Hugh playing guitar.

It happened at lunchtime. We met in a bar. Josephine, the secretary, was there, and Michael, the junior partner. Those were the days, in St Albans.

Mr Nottage came in. He was looking for a negotiator to wheel and deal for football teams, someone to buy stars. Imagine buying Fàbregas, or David Beckham!

"I've only been to one in my whole life," I laughed, "and I don't understand the offside rule, so I'd be no good at that!"

He pulled up a chair, slid closer.

"What are you drinking?"

That's when Hugh moved in: "You're not having her; she's our star!"

(I'd just sold 22, The Park. Hugh's blonde hair looked slick under the spotlights.)

He interrupted the order: "She's being polite – she only drinks Bollinger."

Ray left subdued, and ruffled.

The gig was in a pub, not far from Serpentine Wood. Hugh played 'Hotel California', his voice dark and gritty. He dedicated a song, and did I want to sing?

"Don't marry Colin, whatever you do!" said his partner.

When it was time for home, Hugh obliged. The smooth, sensual body of the Toyota cut through like a night bird.

"I'd like to see you," he whispered, "on your own." He put his arm round my waist. "No one must find out!" And so, we made our bond.

"Meet me at King's Cross," a familiar voice said, years later.

It was winter; I wore a scarlet coat. You noticed it once, in the lecture theatre. You mentioned that song, a song about a lady you hardly knew.

They say: "That was intentional. You were the dancer. "

I wore a showstopper gown, black mesh stockings, red stilettos and a black silk scarf. "We're going on a mystery tour near the Palace," my lover said in his off-duty voice, which gave off a suggestion of controlled excitement. He tied the scarf to make a blindfold, and guided me through the loitering, sweaty crowds to a Hackney cab.

"It's been like torture since the last time," Hugh revealed as he removed the blindfold, and kissed my face in full view of surprised bystanders clustered round the doors which led to a stylish nouvelle cuisine restaurant. We were at London's smartest hotel. Our room was secluded, at the end of the corridor. Room service delivered a crate of champagne on ice, dinner and flowers.

He went to the bathroom. When he re-emerged his eyes were softened, the pupils dilated, his expression mellow. As if to make the beginning easier, he was turning away, towards the sash window. He opened the curtains. The vista was an oasis of green, illuminated only by lamplight and the distant spectre of a crescent moon.

"Tell me about the doctor – tell me in detail!"

"You're special to me," I said. "You know, it wasn't my mistake."

"I told you not to."

"I know. You are special to me – I need someone and now…"

"Why don't you have your cake and eat it? You always did."

"I wanted to marry him, but to Morley it was a brief encounter. He lacks spontaneity. And he's deeply private. I can't help thinking he looks down on me, thinks I'm not good enough."

"It sounds as if he put his career first."

"He had all the power."

Hugh cleared the glass, and when he turned his face toward me again he said, "Don't say you've fallen for him. Those academic types can't cut it when it comes to real life! I need you, Sue. We'll always see each other, at least promise me that!"

The emergence of a love rival had fuelled his passion. He had Karina. I had always known about her, the girlfriend he'd eventually marry. Her parents dealt in antiques and property, she had money to invest in his business, she was independent. But he hadn't known that I loved Morley, needed stability.

The darkness was my comforter, my lover's profile almost a shadow in the crepuscular light, his hair a halo against the dark maroon leather of an armchair. His eyes were liquid now.

"Was your night beautiful?" he asked.

My story is this: how we rolled naked on a bed of leaves, and the world spun, and we made fire, and we spoke in languages of I and You and Me.

"I'm like water – take me to hear the river by the moor. Here is the secret path, fringed with primroses, eglantine and belladonna. Take me to the river, nowhere else, nowhere left, take me there."

Here we are, on a dark night in an ancient time. I feel the thud of horses' hooves against the earth. The horseman is riding without a saddle, without a bridle. You on your mount, the hooves on the sand, and the white foam: this is where you take me.

The Aftermath

"All you wanted was a fuck!"

"Well now, that is putting it crudely!" He smiles an ironic kind of smile, and laughs a devastating kind of laugh; it makes me feel humbled.

"Tell me why you've decided to dump me!"

"You smoke, for a start!" He observes my reaction, and modifies his answer.

"I've thought about it. You're a very attractive woman. Very attractive. But I'm teaching you. And it's too intense to last. The more I think about it, the more I think it's not a good idea! And there's Felicity…it's not fair, not fair on you or her."

"How did you meet her?"

"On a plane."

I am angry now, and tempted to be sarcastic; mention the mile high club.

"Oh…"

"I've told her about you. It's not fair on you or her. Someone got there first." His smile, respectful and sad now, is consolatory.

"Please, Morley. Don't be boring…"

"I don't date students."

He folds his arms as a barrier. No one can see us at the window, we are so high up. I press my body into him. I am kissing him.

"So you won't give me another chance?"

"Not while I'm still teaching you!"

"Oh, don't you think we could get back together, I mean, see each other in the future?"

"Never say never!"

He shrugs his shoulders, shakes his head and nods. He knows it is time to go. It is time to be alone.

Morley and I are walking along the riverbank, through the memories of our life, lost in our own thoughts and future plans, alone together only in our memories.

"I guess you want it straight again," the hairdresser says, plugging in the GHDs.

They say: "Koreans call that style Niagara." An image in a Venetian mirror of a young Korean girl with violet eyes reminds me of Stephen's Rose.

The stylist's hands are the writer's hands: bony, pigmented artist's hands, caressing waist-length tresses that ripple and shimmer like the river. The water is glass: blue-black, purple and turquoise. The girl's hair is the waterfall. Colours tangle round her waspish waist. Her lover's hard body jostles with hers amongst the hollow, brittle twigs and stones of tumbled amber.

"You know she is a river."(The bass drones.)

They say: "There is chemistry between you."

Stephen's bow-like mouth shudders at Rose's memory. His eyes are the eyes of one who dreams in waking hours. The drone of his voice diminishes. His soft voice voyages beyond his selfhood, as if to reach a long-forgotten territory.

Landscape

Retracing the steps, retracing the years, I took the low road, past the Baptist church where my grandfather used to preach, and on the right was the river, and the caravans with the gypsies.

Nearer town was the bridge, and Bow Street, and next, the promenade with the pier.

The sun was out, the air clear. A man with a green anorak approached me. He spoke in an Irish brogue: "Could you tell me how long it is for the bus to town?"

I knew, but I didn't tell. He might guess I was one of the women. He may have been looking for the traveller woman I'd met.

I varied the route on the return journey home. On the horizon, on the hill, were the library and the university where my father once started medical school. I strolled through the park, past the baths, and scrambled up the pathway, by the babbling river and under the tunnel on to the house.

The occupants were all women. They spent their evenings with their children, doing Welsh crafts: tapestry, cross-stitch, knitting and quilting. I wiled away the hours reading. One lady was a pagan and cast spells.

The Irish traveller had many children. She wondered if I could teach them, but the school wanted a teacher who was fluent in Welsh. They were making the building for the Welsh Assembly, and feeling against the English was still strong. I went to classes. I could remember some prayers, but most of it had gone.

One afternoon the Irish woman and I went swimming. The boys were tetchy and wanted to stay in the pool. It had started to rain, as it only does in Wales, Scotland, Ireland and Cornwall. White sunlight filtered through the low cumulous clouds. We saw a rainbow; it was double, over the mountains, and I thought it was a sign.

"We ought to bless this house, because it's Beltane," said the woman sorceress.

So, at midnight, under a pale watery moon, we spoke the incantation, in both languages. We dropped sea salt at the windows and doorways, and in all four corners of the house. The veil between the two worlds was thin, she told us. And in times past, they gathered flowers, made garlands, and danced round the maypole from dawn to dusk. In times gone, they walked between the fires, lighting up hedgerows and fields of green like beacons in the dark.

I stood on the high road, gazing into the entrance way. The island of trees that had rivalled Kew Gardens for ancient specimens had gone. Where were the birds? I glanced up to the front bedroom window, high up, near the eaves. I imagined I saw a tall, willowy figure, keeping vigil, as if to welcome me. My father, in beige trousers and a check sports jacket, was banging the car door shut, his face beaming from ear to ear as he looked reverently up at Grandmamma, and waved. And my mother, her long, shapely legs swinging round onto the tarmac, her blonde hair buffeting in the breeze, her pink chiffon scarf tangled round her swan-like neck. And my brother, now grown, his legs dangling reluctantly above the ground, as he emerged from the vehicle. He wore blue shorts, a sailor-style T-shirt, Clark's shoes and a light blue baseball cap. He was clutching a newly constructed Lego model. Last of all was myself, my unspent energy bursting out as I took a lungful of sea air and hopped and jumped on the threshold, and rang the round brass bell. "Grandma," I was calling, "we're here!"

The oak door looked smaller from a distance. The house was now a hotel. I could see a white crystal chandelier suspended from the ceiling, like a giant ice sculpture. It was illuminated, and the black and white mosaic in the hallway shone. It resembled a giant chess board.

After all the years, this was a memory Doyle couldn't have. The house was where I returned. In all my haunted imaginings, it was my hiding place: my victory.

The Dance

Cheltenham was cold in winter, and there was snow. I counted
back the years. Ages ago, I thought. Each day I ventured along
the parade, and then took a circular route, into Waterstones.
I headed for the photography section: Ansel Adams, the Gobi
Desert. The photographs were grainy, the sand dunes like giant
breasts. It felt warm, sensuous.

I thought of Reddington and the sari in my wardrobe.
I used to wear it for Diwali, the Festival of Lights. It was red.

"The colour suits you!" they said.

When they dressed me, it was a sort of ceremony, once
a year. They bound the material round my body, painted my
hands in elaborate patterns; mehndi, as they do at weddings.
They placed a small red dot at the centre of my forehead. As
I walked, silver bangles made music on my wrists, like the
wind across the desert.

Sometimes I caught a glimpse of Somalian women in High
Meadows. They were Amazonian; graceful, in flowing robes.
Their children surrounded them. They always traversed the
city in groups, and seldom hurried.

Springtime came, and the flowers. Jayne told me of a secret
archway, under the Regency apartments; it led to Cheltenham
Ladies' College. One day, a foreigner was standing near the
entrance. I went ahead, taking a swift glance over my shoulder.
I never used to do that. He caught up with me as I rushed
down the hill.

"Are you all right?" he asked. "You look a bit lost!"

He had a French accent – Lyon, not Paris.

"You have a good body," he said.

He was ten years my junior, judging from his appearance. He volunteered he was returning soon. He was employed in the hotel industry. At the bottom of the hill we parted ways. I wished him bon voyage with a smile of relief on my face.

Black and White

I've bought a notebook again, for my writing. On the front cover there's an expression that my students and I love: "People like to see Nature in the raw."

I've bought paper, too, and a pen. Writing is social; it's an intimate relationship.

When I write, I write to fine-tune. I open the piano, examine the hammers, blow down the dust, and stroke the felts. I want the pictures in my mind to unfold. Before I write, I have an idea I need to discover.

"Where do we go from here?"

I wanted to stay with you, hold you to my breasts. But I was unready– now I know.

When I'm writing there are interludes, writings over, obliterations, scribbles, insertions. Things said by the way, in passing; spillages, slips.

It's performative, a process, a journey we take together, about flow, feelings, rhythm, timing. On the computer the 'thingness' of it invisibly shifts me forward. The screen lacks shadow, rummaging in the corners. It dazzles and obfuscates; there are no subtleties.

The thingness of the machine drives me from A to B, like on the Underground in the capital, with a driver I do not know. I can't say to him, "Stop, I forgot to say I love you to the man standing on the platform at Fulham or South Kensington, the one with the dark hair, greying now, and the magnetic green eyes, and the voice, and the snort when he laughs, and the red scarf."

I buy a ticket for some predetermined destination that some

official thinks I want to go to. We arrive on time or thereabouts. I sit or stand with every random passenger who cares to take this route. "Mind the gap!" the cut-glass crystal-clear voice instructs. And I recall the uniform stations, the standard billboards, advertisements for the average man shouting back at the moving windows. And people on the platform always stand in front of them, like novice teachers at the whiteboards. There is something about a screen, a wall or a window that says, "It's okay! Stand in front of me, obscure what I say, interrupt me, talk over my head, let things pop up in my space – the machine does!"

I guess it must be the Embankment.

Someone stands at a sign, in my line of vision. My body's forced forward by the momentum of the machine, even when it stops. My being is stranded, my brain overridden, left hanging there in space. It makes you want to draw air.

You miss the paraphernalia of writing, the special places you prepare. Writing is worship, a ceremony, a ritual. You miss the anticipation as your fingers touch the sheets, as you trace the watermarks: hidden secrets. You miss the decadent silkiness of it, the glide of it, as your hand warms the pen; the deep swoop and surge of ink. You miss the deep digging corrections of the tip, the scratch below the surface. Writing is like creating tattoos which are invisible, under your skin. You miss the notes, the dribbles and leakages. You miss the fingerprints of saliva, marking the territory of where you've been, the satisfaction of saying, when only your lover is here, the zip of the case as you take out our pen.

You miss the scribble in the sandpit, the liquid clay of it, the plasticine shapes, the scratch and paw at the borders, the play of it, and the *jouissance.*

Show me the ecstasy and pain, the incantation that accompanies the birth – "Push harder, push harder!"

And you send me into bringingdownthewalls. I cry. I howl. The pages begin to drop. And the darling flutters, tumbles; my baby, don't blink now, head first.

Journeys

"I shouldn't have told about your eyes!" the journalist said.

He was clean-cut, blonde, with a cool temperament; sometimes he reminded me of Bjorn Borg. He was totally at ease; nothing fazed him. He could be an idiot, I suppose, and get away with it by doing nothing.

"My parents want to meet you," he said.

It didn't help I had the nickname Eliza; we'd met by a flower stall in Covent Garden. I always felt inferior, as if my background wasn't as good as his. If he had a quality I envied, it was his precision with things, though he made social faux pas. He could do as he liked; it was a God-given birthright.

He was a writer; he had a fantastic eye. The copy layout was all done by hand, and then by courier to the printers, or in person, to Liverpool, by the docks. Sometimes I helped him write. He was good at technicalities, first time round. I was slapdash. Sometimes I envied him his job. He was weak at interviewing; a typical only child, he lacked empathy.

I felt nervous the first time I met them. Leafy avenues of 1950s houses with suburban gardens and the faint hum of sit-on lawnmowers greeted me. His father had striking blue eyes, and a Home Counties voice. He portrayed an air of quiet self-assurance, as he extended a confident hand. His mother was elegant. She greeted me, and went to make coffee. I admired the fields at the back, beyond the rhododendrons and azaleas.

"They're not fields, they're the garden!" Colin's father said.

He surveyed me, up and down.

"It's true about your eyes!" he chortled.

He had a quiet, upper class charm. In that instant, I liked him. In the kitchen, I felt I'd found a kindred spirit. Phoebe told me she loved art.

"Do you like music?" I asked her.

"Well," she said, speaking into the distance (I could hear the Bow bells in her voice), "I never have!"

She was someone who didn't like music. We would have very little to talk about, I thought. I believe she was sulking.

I cannot be bitter about Colin. He was clean, methodical and organised. What he lacked in spontaneity he made up for in planning, until the mistake.

"I'm going to be late on Friday."

"Work?"

I was in the kitchen, throwing coconut milk into the wok.

"No," he said. "I'm meeting a friend, from Peru." (The face seemed to be inscrutable, but I have an ear, sometimes, for these things: a tightening of the voice, a pitch, reverting to monotone.)

"They." (The sobriquet covered it, he thought.)

"Have you known them long?"

The dish needed more curry paste; it was bland.

"I met them on a walking holiday."

"Where are you going to meet them?"

"I want to show them the sights of London."

Our eyes met.

"Is she just a friend?"

"Yes," he stalled. His back was turned away from me. He stood at the kitchen window, which faced the patio and a raised wall with an herbaceous border. Grey-green rosemary spilled over onto the yellowish stone. "Oh, you didn't think…?"

"No, not for one minute…"

"I love you," he reassured. The blue eyes momentarily met mine, and then flew to a target in the distance.

The second time was soon after. Ties tell tales. Unbuttoned

shirt collars. He'd missed the last train. He looked drained. He looked hot. He hadn't said anything about the tour. I knew.

We'd sent out invitations, we'd booked the hotel. It had a lake with water-lilies, perfect for the photos; his friend was going to take them. My cousins from Ireland were flying over. And my mum and Julian would be there. I couldn't be seen to fail, so I went ahead regardless.

I thought of a happier time, at Dunkery Beacon on a clear spring day. "Will you marry me?" he whispered, kneeling to the side of me, the words warming my ear. I felt giddy. "I'll think about it," I said. I could see the clear horizon in the distance. There would be time to go anywhere, do anything. The future seemed to be limitless then.

"Were you happy before you met him?" Vanessa asked.

I knew she'd understand. She'd had piercings and tattoos, her armour against cultural constraints. "Look!" she seemed to say, "This is who I am."

The marriage was magical, in places, I told her. He called me *mooie vlinder*—pretty butterfly, in Dutch. We were in Copenhagen on our honeymoon, in Nyhavn, where the boats and the sea and the beautiful people go. "Why don't you have a tattoo," he said, "on your inner thighs, or flying above the little garden, with the flowers?" I ejaculated there and then. His words were erotic, mysterious. I could transform my body, myself.

The parlour was like the dentist's, with a black leather chair. Elaborate illustrations were on the walls. "Is there anything special you'd like?" said the man with illustrated, hairless arms.

"She wants a butterfly," Colin said. I saw the needle and I fainted. They carried me through the rain to a waiting car. My skin was soaked.

In the bedroom of the Hans Christian Andersen Hotel:

"What happened?"

"You turned into a butterfly!" he murmured, "And I'm going to chase you!"

"That's unusual for a guy," Vanessa said. "He was so imaginative…What was he like in bed?"

I remember the chalet house abroad. There were fires of applewood in winter. The aroma was wondrous. The flames were flickering, caressing our bodies. I imagined it was Norway or Sweden. The log cabin had snow peaking against the grainy timber. Outside were wolves. We were safe. We were warm.

His eyes were wonderfully blue, like his father's. As I looked into the fires, I saw a dark stranger. He was older, an accomplished rider, and I was in love with him. He was the love from a past, from long, long ago.

A spectral snowy owl came into view one autumn evening, on the road to Fotheringhay, along by the river, where Mary, Queen of Scots had escaped. The bird was magnificent, with piercing talons; its plumage was like feather down, the wings both strong and delicate. The feathers were luminous.

I never had the tattoo. But when the lilacs came, that's when I saw it; when the buddleia bush was in full bloom with dark purple flowers that's when I saw it first: a butterfly with paint-box wings, a Red Admiral. It dizzied about the flowers, intoxicated by a first taste of honey.

I'll always remember Colin. I loved his sensitive side, his femininity. He wrote me a letter which I lost on my journey. We'd betrayed each other, but some things would remain forever.

"I harbour no grudge against you," he wrote. "I'll always remember the happy times we had. I have been doing some simple walks, spending time less sociably than you, I suspect. I hope you meet someone you love, who will sustain you. The most beautiful things in this world are often the most fragile."

When the Italian returned from the sun, that's when I knew.

"I've got this for you!" he said.

Antonio handed me a discreet package in white tissue paper. The butterflies were made of blue crystal, and were delicate. The Italian smiled a warm, meaningful smile. I gave him a faraway, wistful look. How thoughtful he was, I felt. He'd remembered my story, and the lines of Audrey Hepburn: "You can always tell what kind of person a man really thinks you are by the earrings he gives you."

(I didn't let on I knew, for that would spoil the mystery.)

Who is my companion on my journey through the dark night of the soul? Is there any light in the shadows? There was once a train journey, a journey past the graveyard with my father's ashes. There are flowers at the trackside, bright wreaths, and I am drawn into a long tunnel, into the pitch black and the shadows. I see a tall, slender figure beckoning me. The train continues, getting closer and closer to the centre of all things. Then, the beautiful figure in a white flowing gown at the end of the tunnel turns away from me.

"I want to see him again, be close to him and those who have gone."

"She's not ready," they say.

I know I have returned, to draw breath. I see a white light at the tunnel's end, melting like time in Dali's clocks.

It was time for Latin, time for mathematics, and I was AWOL. They probably wouldn't notice.

I loved to go, alone. Crawl under the rolling stage door in the vast assembly hall, and get out through the escape hatch. Over the playing fields I ran, past the goal posts, and clambered over the gate by the fence and onto the backstreets. They brought me out beyond the perimeters.

Breathless now, I stood in the tunnel by the train tracks reading graffiti. There were hollow voices when you shouted. I loved to be alone; it was monotonous, a waking dream.

I entered the cemetery. The last time I'd been there I'd taken my dog. Where were the ashes? I couldn't find them; I couldn't find the place. Regulations had been followed, unmarked by any stone. I think the spaniel knew, though.

When we got to the place he howled. But today, all was silent. I wished that his ashes had been scattered, off a promontory, into the ocean, or by a river, with sedge grass, luminescent in the moonlight as feathers in the sand.

I stood motionless for a moment, and spoke a silent prayer. Then on to the park and by the black river and the willows which festooned the banks. I'd nearly drowned there once.

The sun came out, warm on my back through my white school blouse. The streets were familiar, past the old tannery, the Jet garage. Past the Asian corner shop with rainbow jars of Kayli, gobstoppers and sherbet love hearts. I was in love with Frankie. My father had said, "He's got his head screwed on!" But he was Bev's brother, and just a chaperone.

I drifted past the library, dragging my leather satchel, past Roses' dress shop where I worked. I might be there on Wednesdays, too, if teachers didn't notice. Then past the old mill and the circular return. It was nearly home time, time to meet my brother off the coach from school.

Sometimes my mother came back on time, sometimes late. I looked after Julian as best I could. Nothing was the same anymore. He took a radio apart and re-assembled it again; he understood how things worked. Sometimes, this was very useful. He knew how magnets could slow the march of electricity meters. A kindly neighbour, a car mechanic, took him under his wing. By the age of ten, he understood how to repair an engine in the way a skilful surgeon might heal a heart. But in his dark moods, he broke things.

The house was now unrecognisable. Subtle colours, gentle on the eye, colours my father had favoured, were replaced by louder, clashing schemes. The black French papier mâché table with white mother-of-pearl butterflies and flowers disappeared. There were more visitors, all of a sudden. There was no quiet: my mother got drunk, and my brother hit out. My sensibilities were jarred. The voices came, the voices, the voices – the hangers-on.

I used to sit alone, planning things, planning how to get out.

"So where did you go?" Vanessa asked, taking a thoughtful draw on a spliff.

"I went to work in a hotel – I was a receptionist. It was a live-in job."

The journey to Easton Hall went past the barracks where my father had worked. At the entrance of the camp I could see the security post with the guards. Minutes passed. I had arrived at the hotel, where I would stay.

It was midnight when she came. The porter, the waiter and the dancing girls had finished for the night. The porter, a short, stunted man with the look of a seafarer said, "Arr, in a minute, look, she'll be 'ere. She always walks, look, dead on twelve. Yarl see. There she goes!" He tugged at my sleeve. "She's very light, look, on her feet."

My company that evening turned their faces towards me. In the pale green light of the lamp, which played upon the caverns of his face, I noticed, for the first time, the sadness in his eyes.

"There she goes, look," he whispered, nudging me. The apparition swept through the corridor, through the heavy fire doors, which swung open of their own accord. I yawned, and followed, to my bed.

Summer came and went. I returned home; my mother answered the bell. "Why are you wearing my things?" She stood in the glass front porch, wearing the flower-print top and skirt in delicate pastels – my clothes.

"I thought you weren't coming back." When I went to the room with the hockey sticks plaque, my brother's Airfix had been moved there. I took the guest room instead.

"So where did you go the next time, when you really left?" Vanessa said, pouring me a glass of Chardonnay.

"Birmingham."

"What, on your own?"

"Yes," I said, "I was nearly eighteen then."

The hostel was on Bristol Road, near the cinema. A young Malaysian woman called Zinee, maybe twenty-one or so, taught me how to make pancakes. "It's not safe here," she said. "A girl was murdered last year in the laundry room." We clung together; there was still talk of the bombings.

I liked my job, and then I was bored. The best time was at Heathrow Airport Hotel. We had a fancy dress party, by the swimming pool. There were limbo dancers, jugglers, fire-eaters and a steel band. People were thrown in the water, but no one was drunk. The next day we were at Sales School. "People don't buy products," they told us. "They buy people and dreams!"

That year I sold a lot of cosmetics. Little spider veins appeared on my legs – nothing much. We had to stand. But the music played, and it was ABBA, and I was curious about love. We often met after work. I went to a party at Christmas, at Judy's house. I was the baby of the group; they liked Donna Summer.

Breaking Away

I was just nineteen when I married. We'd met in The Chase. He was a Pharmacology major, a man of sensitivity, Roman Catholic, a man of extremes.

"I don't know what you see in him!" Susan said.

"I thought you were going to college," said Alison.

Julie said, "He's not for you!"

But I was headstrong then, I wouldn't listen to reason.

I remember the first time I saw him he wore shades. He had a friend, Ralph, who worked on oil rigs. They both looked like cowboys, in faded jeans and leather boots and jackets.

I was working at a bank; I'd been there two years. First, I was a cashier, then my chance came and I was a marketing and promotions girl, one of six in the country. One day, we went to a basketball match: Team Fiat, in Derby. The local press came and captured the moment. The players towered over me as I presented the winner's trophy.

At the speedway event, Ole Olsen won. Who dared to go on the victory lap? I would. I adored the rush of wind against my skin and the roars of the crowd. As the machine leaned forty-five degrees they held their breath and shrieked.

My manager followed me to the VIP stand.

"You were great, Sue!" he gushed.

He followed me to the table with champagne glasses. I could feel his eyes crawling over me as I balanced a plate of Marmite Twiglets and salmon and cucumber sandwiches.

"Don't take any notice of Dad," his daughter giggled, "he's going through a mid-life crisis!"

One evening though, he came to my rescue. I was going to Foleshill, to promote bank accounts at the Liberal club, that was all. But Greg was furious.

At 7pm, there was a knock at the door. I opened it halfway.

"Okay?" he said.

I was shaking my head.

"Tell you in the car."

There were two inner doors, broken off their hinges on the floor.

"I see you've had the builders in," he said.

I was grateful for his diplomacy.

"I can't remember him," Vanessa said, a furrow on her brow.

"You were young then."

"Sue," she said. "If you get married again, can I be bridesmaid!"

"You never know, I like wedding cake!"

She knew, I think, what I intended. She'd heard from Brian, the handsome one in Dublin. He liked the single life these days; he'd just come out of the closet.

"I may live with someone, but I'd have to know them, really know them first!"

"But does anyone really ever know anyone?"

"We all live behind masks," I said, "but some have integrity."

"What is your definition of that?" She sounded like the professor.

"I mean having a sense of wholeness; a person who decides on the right thing to do when no one else is looking, someone who has a kind of core, a moral centre."

"Some of the things I've regretted the most are things I did when I was high or drunk!"

"I don't regret the things I did when I was drunk," I said, "just how I did them; the way I behaved, the things I said."

(The object of my adoration returns, in memory.)

"Why won't you see me?"

"It's the things you say, the way you act."

"Is there a chance we could get back together?"

"Never say never!"

His face suggests it's all a big joke. I am frozen to the spot, I cannot move. Useless. Arguing. Futile. There are tears of frustration running down my face. He puts the kettle on. Passes me a tissue. Always practical, always cool in a crisis, just like my father was.

"Oh?"

Vanessa's gaze is scrutinising; her ear is turned towards my mouth, as if she is waiting.

"I wanted to hold him." I spew the words out.

"Unfinished business?"

There is a silence between us, and I'm aware of time slipping away, slipping away beyond my reach, with the march of a clock.

"I guess you could call it that. But he'd meet a different me from the one he met then."

Vanessa shifted from the couch. She stood momentarily at the side window, which had a vista of a mossy walled garden where ferns grew in earthenware pots.

Be still and know. That was the motto on the university crest at Sussex. It was at St Albans Abbey in the Verulamium Park. I was thinking about Si's funeral service, and how the rich quality of Doyle's baritone voice as he sang failed to betray the inner character. So voices were masks, masks were a dance, dancing with each other, masks were echoes.

How small I was, gazing at the rose window in the north transept, observing the beauty of the colours which changed with the angle of the sun. Vanessa was by my side. I was reliving the walks with Colin. Ice skaters were gliding and twirling across the frozen lake, and tobogganers in brightly coloured woollens were hurtling down the slopes. At the centre of the park was the river, and The Fighting Cocks pub, the oldest pub in England, where we drank mead and toasted in the New Year. In springs and summers the park was excavated as archaeologists searched for what remained, interpreting evidence and making their story.

He says, "A knight in armour walks the abbey grounds, along a path long gone, and disappears."

Years had passed, but I felt a sense of ontological security. We were gazing together at history. We were living in the moment. As we stood bathed in pools of colour, I wondered how many others had gazed at the window, and what they saw. Later, in the abbey shop, Vanessa bought a gargoyle.

Transformations

Yesterday I had a long lunch with Pearl, my Korean friend.

"I'm having a pyjama party," she said.

"I haven't got any pyjamas or nightdresses!"

"So what do you wear?"

"Number 5," I said, joking. "I won't come in the raw, I promise!"

Stephen had asked her if he could come. A challenge brings out the actor in him. He begs. His eyes are those of a spaniel when the turkey is being prepared at Christmas.

"No!" she said firmly. "Girls only!"

This morning she gave me a carrier bag of face masks and an apple.

"Your skin will look beautiful!" she said.

I have a theory about synchronicity. The universe knows a transformation is underway.

I remember the second or third time I left. I was standing near the statue of Thomas Cook, near the rail station, phoning a helpline.

"Can you get to St Albans?" they said.

Days later, I met Jayne.

She was tall and gangly, with an elfin face and a warm heart. When I first arrived, I never took off my coat, even indoors. It was winter, but mild that year.

"It was your comfort blanket," she said.

All I cared about was survival then. She told me about her life. There were parallels; that's how I learnt.

She'd lived in Cornwall as a child. She was a stargazer,

a dreamer. Her father was a fisherman. When he died, she never had closure. He'd disappeared one night in a storm. A search party did all they could, but at sunrise they couldn't find any trace of him. Word went round that the sea had taken him.

I remember one morning I was fast asleep in my bed. She didn't speak, she sang.

"Wake Up Little Susie."

It was my father's voice. The words vibrated in my heart, lifting my spirits, like a distant chord sent from angels.

"We won't tell anyone!" Pearl said, locking her finger in mine to seal the promise. She was telling me of the love she'd lost; perhaps there was no hope, after all. I told her that the fifties was a good decade for some people. The corners of her thin mouth were downturned, and she tapped the coffee cup on the rim of the saucer, nervously. It was a sad affair. "I've lived with someone all my life, but haven't loved him. He's a good provider." Privately, I considered myself lucky.

"I married anyone who was important to me," I later confessed to Stephen. And that was almost true. Over my shoulder, in the periphery of my vision, Imogen, the European platinum blonde who studied for a doctorate, beautiful, tragic Imogen, who'd never married, was laughing triumphantly behind her hand.

The Awakening

"How very English of you!" she said.

I was in her kitchen diner, drinking latte at the breakfast bar. The woman was Bartholomew's aunt. We'd just come off a flight with Freddie Laker; we were exhausted. When she spoke I felt vulnerable, and blushed.

The house was rather grand, I thought. The rooms were large, a diner at the hub. There was a lounge with triple aspect windows, a lobby and a downstairs rest room. Five bedrooms were at the top of a central staircase, which had a galleried landing; I liked that best of all.

His aunt was in her early fifties, vibrant, with hazel eyes and Titian hair. "Lawrence will be home at three," she announced. He worked in a supermarket, stacking shelves. I visualised him meeting me for the first time. I was glad I'd worn my stockings, although it was hot.

He was short and chubby, with a ruddy, sunburnt complexion. "Welcome to the United States!" he said, shaking his cousin's hand, nodding at me in acknowledgement. I hugged my coffee close, and studied my feet. Bartholomew looked jaded from the plane journey, more like the bank clerk he was. "Where do you guys wanna visit?" Lawrence asked. I knew I wanted to visit Hollywood, but I'd never considered Las Vegas. "I have a pickup truck. Gail and Nigel can ride in the two-seater. It may be cold, but you guys will be okay with a blanket."

That weekend there was a thunderstorm over Sunset Strip. The hotel lights failed, just as I was taking a shower. We made up and dressed in the dark. Then we went to Caesar's Palace; The Four Tops were singing.

The casino lounge was luxurious, with men who walked like penguins in dinner suits. Women in sheath dresses dealt cards as if it were a matter of life and death. The wheel spun round. We lost. Barry knew the game was up. A promotions girl, dressed like a white rabbit, gave us coupons for a cafe round the block.

In the back room there were one-armed bandits. An old spinster turned over dimes in her liver-spotted hand, a rolled cigarette drooping from her thin mouth. The tobacco spilled untidily from the untipped end, smoke thickening the atmosphere, which was tinged with brown-yellow, matching the off-white patched-up walls. We found somewhere else, and then we returned to the little shack on the edge of the desert.

Sunday evening was so welcoming. Bartholomew's aunt was warm and earthy, like those from the Midwest. At the dinner table she played the mother matriarch, and everyone said grace together. She called me Bartholomew's fiancée, though I wasn't. It was respectable to them; they were avidly religious, but wine was still served at the table.

Pamela wore a beautiful nightdress, in pure white chiffon. Just before bedtime, she was dancing in the half-light on the landing, as if it were a stage. This was her moment to shine. On the gramophone was a love song; it was Elvis. In my mind's eye, I saw my mother then. For the first time, she was a separate being from me, but that's another story, in Italy.

I can see my mother now. Her peach-like complexion glowed as she descended the stairs into the marble hall. The champagne flute seemed to be fixed in her curled hand. As she threw her head back, Medusa-like as if to laugh, I saw the concierge, his head on the desk.

I rang the bell; it was 1am. And as he stirred, I saw it was not a dress but a diaphanous negligee. I spoke to her. And then she turned away, the sheen on the skin of her back glimmering in the afterglow. A vision in black, she was ascending once more, her footfall lightly, softly fading, until there was no sound at all.

The night cradled my soul, as I listened to the faint tick of electric on the cable. I thought of Roberto, and the rose, the Stork nightclub where we'd danced. And the idea came: she was lost, and in the morning we'd be going home.

One evening it was just me and Lawrence. We were talking about religion and Nostradamus, and the end of the world. "It'll be a conflict between the super-powers," he said, "Russia and China. One of the countries was symbolised by The Bear."

"The thing is, why is there so much conflict, suffering and war in the world, if there is a benign God?"

Lawrence was getting excitable.

"Holy smoke! Humans make bad choices. God gives them free will."

It was getting late, and he was due at work.

"I'm gonna be late tonight," he told his employers on the telephone. "I'm having a talk about God with Susan!"

(It could only happen in America.)

I think the family thought we'd marry in the White Chapel Hall. "I'll sponsor you to stay in the States," Pamela said. "Rubin would agree to it!" Rubin was her ex-husband, a psychoanalyst, and they were now friends. Bartholomew let me decide. But I was heading home; we could live together in Britain. I was going to be a recruitment consultant.

We went to Disneyland and Santa Monica on the coast.

"Go blonde!" they cooed. "Get a suntan – you'll be the all-American girl!"

"We love that British accent!"

The Colour of Money

He sat behind a highly polished desk, in an office with no pictures. There were no filing cabinets that I remember. His shoes were black slip-ons. I think he wore striped socks. His feet were squarely positioned on the carpet-tiled office floor. He rarely moved his hands as he talked, except when he steepled them. His eyes seemed to cut right through you. There was a name plate on his desk. 'Do it now!' it said. (He claimed he lived by those words to the letter.) "Right!" he said, in a broad Yorkshire accent, "while you're sat 'ere I'm to meck an urgen phorn call!"

Minutes later, in came his sidekick. The opposite of himself, he looked like Lionel Blair, on a good day. He was a dandy, I thought. "What I want you to knors you got tut think you're the best bugger there is, or else forget it, in this business," the boss said, his face quite stern now.

"I am!" I quipped. (Oh, the arrogance!)

"Well then," the dandy chimed in, "we should think about hiring her!"

"I'll let you knor int morning," the big man said.

And when I got up, the air expelled from the low chair, that had farted when I sat.

I learnt a great deal from him. He criticized me early on. He thought I didn't suffer fools gladly, but didn't need to tell them exactly, like Benjamin Franklin. He handed me a book entitled *How to Win Friends and Influence People*.

"Read it," he ordered, "and shor me you 'ave! I 'orp we'll be seeing some subtlety int future, but dorn be going soft on me

186

eh? You'll still be callin' spade a spade, as far as I'm concerned."

I was pleased when he promoted me a year later.

"Now you control all contracts for the City and Old Street," he told me. "What do you think? Tell me straight!"

"Can I smoke?" I asked. (Oh, the weakness!)

On one further condition, that I had an ashtray in my office, I accepted.

"Ah, you're 'ard," he joked, "but don't forget who made you!"

The receptionist at my base was attractive, in a deliciously common way. She had long, cheaply blonded hair and olive skin. She was big-breasted, about 38E. Clients seemed to come out of nowhere to see her. "Nowone comes to see me," she whined one day. "When they talk to me, they 'ave a conversation with me tits!"

When she was in this mood, her voice was faster and more Brummie, and the ends of sentences were so high pitched they may well have shattered windows. Then she met a guy on a train to London. He was a diamond merchant. She wanted to marry him, so she mellowed.

I worked hard. I got results. Then, one day, the big man called me on the phone from his nearby office.

"You 'avin a good day, eh? Busy, eh?"

"Yes," I said.

"Well, I'll tell yer now, it's going t' be even better for talkin' t' me! Get your arse down tut station. I'd gor meself, but I'm sending you as a proxy. Sort it out at Oxford Street for me, will yer, eh? They're not doin' the bloody figures, an' I for one want to know what the 'eck's goin' on! You'll be writin' me a full report. And if they're pissing about, sack 'em, right? Get your arse on the next bloody train, eh! I want you there as soon as possible. Get yourself checked in tut hotel when you get there. You can phone that man, Bart is it, whatsisname, and let him knor, eh? You'll be down there at least a week, right, all expenses paid – and booze, if you want it, on me! Now you can't moan at that, can yer, eh? What d'yer say? You'll do it for me? Grand! Get your arse down that station, now!" The phone clicked off.

Oxford Street overwhelmed me. It was so busy. I checked into a hotel for businesspeople. In the morning, I made my debut. They didn't know what my mission was.

"I've come to help out," I said.

He'd given me some categories under which I'd assess them: timekeeping, sales approach, motivation, results, and charisma, whatever that was.

In the afternoon, a man with an expensive Savile Row suit approached me at my desk.

"Hi," he said, straightforwardly, "I'm Mrs Hurst's son."

I told him I'd read her autobiography, *No Glass Slipper*, and how I admired what she had done.

"Let's go to Chelsea and Kensington tonight," he suggested, "and get to know each other better over dinner!" That took me by surprise.

"Did thee try to poarch ya," the big man snarled on my return.

"Mm, kind of."

"Eee, I thought thee would."

His steel-grey eyes were narrowing, focusing on me and then the report, which he held up into the light.

"So what is it that's sor different about them soft southerners, eh?" Then he added, "You're not one of 'em are ya, eh?"

I couldn't be dishonest with him, and so I replied: "I don't identify with anywhere in particular, I'm a typical midlander!"

We discussed the report, the hard sell and the soft sell. I favoured the latter every time.

"Selling people a job is like selling dreams," I said. "They've got to want the opportunity, so they give their best. Once we get quality candidates, we can build our client base. A good standard of service will always get repeat business; that's what's wrong in Oxford Street. Interviewers don't understand how to create a need; they need to talk to people by painting pictures, with words that are persuasive. Candidates are always looking for a benefit, something they've never had. We need to make them reach for it. It's all about the psychology of selling – someone should teach the interviewers that!"

"Eee," he said. He was leaning back in his chair, as if to view me as an object. I hoped that I was glittering; a star on which he could project his every ideal, his every fantasy of the perfect executive.

"He thinks your eyes are like the blonde in "*Dallas!*" Zelda said, with a roll of her eyes and her soft feminine smile. "Use it!"

The big man made a sudden drumming noise on the surface of the desk, as if he had decided.

"You'll be going down to Oxford Street again," he said, "an' I 'ope you'll teach'em. We 'aven't got much time, right, an' I want you back 'ere as soon as possible. We'll be meckin an Area Manager of you yet. But I need to know you can deliver, right. Now one thing I want you to knor – if they're not right, I mean 'opeless case, you won't be mecking anything of them, thee won't change, right!"

I had just three weeks to 'sort 'em', or three of the ten would be getting fired.

King Henry the Eighth Hotel was nothing special. The rooms were plain, comfortable and functional. The saving grace, perhaps, was the restaurant.

The head waiter breathed life into the place. The job suited him. He remembered my room number at the breakfast table. He knew that I liked my croissants warm, not hot, and that I enjoyed burnt toast. He brought me extra thin cut marmalade.

There was occasional hassle from other customers, men cruising hotels on overnight business stops, who smelt of strong cologne and mouthwash. They treated you as a person who could be bought. How much better it is now for the modern woman, networking on the Internet. I can imagine it: any other women in Paris this morning? Meet me at this hotel, that restaurant; safety in numbers.

At the office, I watched and waited to make my move. I paid the interviewers three compliments for every negative, and one of them was cured. "Ditch the Half Nelson!" I told her. I learnt that one from Ron the Con, my mother's super-salesman boyfriend. "The only person who doesn't expect to be conned is a con!" That was his favourite saying. "Offering a choice of two doesn't work," I advised. "Southerners are urbane – a choice of two won't make them bite!"

I thought of the waiter in the restaurant. His artistry made evenings at the restaurant magical: flowers were blended with linen in subdued pastels, silver trays and Oneida cutlery sparkled, crisp white napkins were folded like lotus flowers, the glasses gleamed in the light of taper candles. The head waiter didn't mind if you lingered over the menu, fingered the gold-leaf pages, and took time to decide.

To tell you the truth, it was horribly lonely. In the solitary evenings, I speculated where Bart might be. I filled the insecurity of silences with talk, phoning him to boost my confidence. I was dizzy, my judgement clouded from the wine. One night I cried, "Everyone wants a piece of me!" I felt like a trinket; something insubstantial, shallow, all surface.

When I returned to the northern city, my mentor was in a jovial mood. He was satisfied with my update. He'd approved of the tape recordings. "Eee, they only made one of you," he said, pouring the spilt black coffee from the saucer back into the cup. "But with them recordings thee warnt forget 'ow it's done!"

He pulled a printout from his slim briefcase.

"Did you like 'otel?" he enquired. A flicker of amusement moved across his lips.

"Yes, not bad," I said.

"What was the restaurant like?"

He listened intently.

"Oo else was there? Lorn le was it, eh?"

Then he read out the numbers; there were several. He was in full flow.

"Oo's this guy, 0203 117 9654?"

He was laughing now.

"Oor, and again! Three hours this time! What the 'eck were you talking about, eh? You dornt avter ansa me! And again! Are you marrying 'im or something? Again! 'E's popular! Bart is it, eh? 'E must 'ave some talent! Now I knor you like meckin phorn calls. But one 'undred and fifty pounds and twenty-seven pence! It's a lot of monnee, right? I'll pay 'alf, what d'yer say, eh? Is that fair?"

I looked him in the eyes. He'd got me rumbled. I felt the heat rise in my complexion. At that moment, he reminded me of my father. I thanked him, got up from the chair. I didn't want to let him down, but I couldn't drive yet.

"He wants to put on a production in the West End," Zelda, the manager, said fondly, twisting the chain on her monogrammed silver locket. There were rumours about her, but I didn't believe them. It was jealousy.

"Are you going to act?" she said.

I thought of the exposure. I'd rather be in the back room, writing the words.

"I'll do the script writing!" I enthused.

I wanted to get a team together.

"Don't you want to act?" Mr W said, breathing dramatically down the mouthpiece. He must have been in the boardroom; there was an echo.

"No," I returned, "I don't have time, but I may write a few words."

"The theme is women's emancipation," he said. "We're looking for something fresh and dynamic that goes with the image of our company!"

SJM was a close ally in the endeavour. She was a Celt, from Scotland. She didn't like chauvinism; she'd left banking for head-hunting. People said she was a stickler for details, and difficult. She swore like a man. "Balls," was her favourite expletive, and she called idiots "Dickhead!" But I thought she had a brain and a half. And I liked the dizzy blonde who'd been to America, training Harvard style. Her name was Day; Dizzy Day we called her, and she was imaginative and creative.

"There's something about three," Elaine said years later, and I understood. With three there were more possibilities for closeness and distance, the ever-changing gap; a dynamic for envy, competition, twists, turns, desire, seduction. We spent weekends in Mansfield together. 'Writers' Weekends' we called them. I fell in love with the idea, and almost became someone else.

"You're always working!" Bartholomew complained. "I never see you these days!" Sadly, the sponsorship was withdrawn –someone had had an argument at the top. Politics had come into it. I have never understood that. I felt a mixture of powerlessness and relief.

("All I needed was the right time, the right team," Doyle had said years later. And I knew how he'd felt.)

"To be honest, Suzanne," Lisa told me earnestly, "when I first met you, I thought you were an airhead, but now I know you're anything but!"

"A bit slow on the uptake, are you!" I quipped.

She saw the funny side of it and chuckled. She's blonde, as well.

We were at a new development called Fabric, studying the copy and photos in my office next to the lap-dancing club. "I'm calling the campaign Bright Lights, Big City," I told her.

"It's your baby!" she said.

*

So what of my journey in estate agency? How had I got there? It was an October morning, at the Midland Hotel in Peterborough. I'd been a Junior Negotiator up to this point. Now I wanted to improve my prospects. I wanted to work for Black Horse Agencies, amongst the best.

The advertising had sold me. I brushed up well for the interview. I wore a navy suit, and a white blouse with a flouncy bow. On arrival, I announced myself at reception. "The interviews are upstairs," the receptionist said, "in a bedroom."

I think I scowled. Was this some kind of initiative test, some kind of joke? Or worse still, a casting couch? I'd said that I was married; that never failed to fend off all-comers, I thought.

I climbed the faded torn carpet on the main stairs, checked the room number. There was nobody outside. Where were the other candidates? I wouldn't go in if there were only girls; that would be some kind of trap.

A young man arrived, walking carefully, his eyes focused on his new shoes.

"Are you from BHA?" he asked me.

"I'm on interview!" I replied.

"It looks odd," he said, "but don't worry. I know one of the guys. His name's Michael."

When my turn came, I crept into the room in the manner of an uninvited guest gate-crashing a party. "Sorry about the room," Michael said. "We booked it in a hurry."

He was very tall and slim, with wiry blonde hair. His eyes were magnetic and bead-like, and very deep blue. He had a manner which suggested seriousness and mirth simultaneously; he was an enigma, until he spoke.

The other guy was portly, with a broad, fleshed-out face, grey collar-length hair, and silver-rimmed glasses. He wore a signet ring. He looked intelligent. He gave up his pink satin

193

upholstered spoon-back chair, and offered me filtered coffee in a china cup with a gold rim and a Turkish pattern. He threw the magenta cushion with the gold tassels on the bed, and held onto it on his lap. He looked awkward, dangling his legs over the side and swinging them as he talked, like a shy guy on a honeymoon. "Shall we start?" Michael said, stifling a belly laugh. (I caught sight of myself in the dressing-table mirror. I looked professional, immaculate, and I smiled.)

Their interview style was ultra-relaxed, to the point of seeming to be incidental; it had the feel of a chat. They improvised questions about St Albans. I supposed that they'd already phoned them. And then came the difficult question, the one for which I had prepared.

"Do you drive?"

"Yes."

I kept it short, sweet, and to the point.

"You have a clean driving licence?" Michael asked, following up.

The way he'd framed the questions couldn't have been better: I held a licence, it was provisional. So the lie was only little, and white – a first ever at an interview.

The job started in January. I had enough time. I'd see Angus that afternoon, I thought. Angus had the jovial appearance of a garden gnome. He was liberal in every sense of the word. Six weeks to learn, from scratch. Maybe we could do it, he thought. One problem was riding the clutch, the other was reversing. There was also a small problem with parallel parking. "If all else fails, just dump it!" he said. "Or hang around, looking helpless. A man will usually oblige, and, any road, it's not part of the test!" I had a few lessons. "Buy a car!" he said.

I bought a Fiat Uno; it was old with go-faster stripes, in red. I'm ashamed to admit I took it into town once or twice before the test. I still couldn't drive. But he knew best.

"Wear your black leather miniskirt!" he suggested.

I laughed. "That's cheating!" I said.

But he persuaded me to do it – others would.

I think my driving was steady enough, and the gears hardly crunched. I nearly stalled the engine once. I pulled out onto a roundabout rather too fast, barely clearing traffic on my right. At the end of the test, I wiped my sweaty palms and braced myself for the worst.

"If you can remember your mistake, you pass," the examiner said.

"I put my foot down at the roundabout and went too fast," I said.

I think he was listening, and he was looking at my face as he handed me the paper; it had worked.

"I've got you a car!" Michael said. It was a new white Vauxhall Nova. I liked the paintwork and the seat covers. There was a mirror on the driver's side for putting on makeup at the traffic lights. I could use the cool air fan for drying my hair when I rose late in the mornings, and there was enough room in the glove compartment for a can of hairspray. Lovely, I thought. "Is there anything you want for the new office?" he said.

"I'll ask the team, and let you know." The staff wanted a fridge and a microwave for lunchtimes so the secretary ordered them. The office was a home from home, domesticated.

I really liked Michael. He was such fun to work with and I could be myself. He and Scott did most of the listing, while the team ran the office. We had breakfast meetings to discuss marketing.

I'd been the day before to value a detached property in a sought-after area. The living rooms were light and airy, there was a games room with a pool and a gym, and there were many bedrooms, all with en-suites. The garden was southerly facing. (I doubt if I'd read the buzzwords anywhere before – I don't think so.) Michael asked me what I thought.

"It really has something special. It has the Wow Factor!" I said.

"What did you just say?" (He wanted to be sure everyone had heard.)

"The Wow Factor!" I repeated.

He wrote the words in a Filofax. "I'm going to use that!" He loved words. They had power.

My sidekick in the office was Sophie. She was a little younger than me and a qualified surveyor. She'd applied for my job, but hadn't succeeded. At first, she gave me a rough ride: she wouldn't cooperate, and sometimes she was aggressive. She watched as I struggled with heavy boxes of stationery. I decide to flex more muscle, but quietly. When I spoke to her, I lowered my voice, to give the impression of restrained anger. "You're either with me, or against me!" I stated bluntly. "This is a team. I'm disappointed!" She apologised, and then gave me the silent treatment. After a difficulty with a chain, when she needed my help, we finally bonded. She backed me up with technicalities that came back from surveys. We complemented each other.

Sometimes Michael and I went out, surveying our little kingdom. "You know, we're all outsiders here," he said. "Not one of us is from Peterborough!"

We got lost together, once, in bad weather.(We'd forgotten the map.)

"Follow the river," I said, "or the train line!"

"That's a really original way of navigating," he said.

(Privately, I thought maps were difficult.)

It was time for corporate advertising in the newspaper. Michael came bounding in, catching his breath. He beamed. Everyone was on the phone. The office was humming. He stood there, in the middle of everything, snapping his red braces. Then there was a lull.

"I'm a Yuppie!" he joked.

Everyone laughed. You felt you'd known him for ages.

"Are you going to get a uniform?"

I looked for Sophie's support. I wanted black suits for the girls, and flattering blouses with bows. Sophie and I had seen a blouse in emerald green – the company colour. It was just right, and Michael approved.

Geoff came in. "Just look at these people who work for me!" Michael said. "They do a good job. Why surround yourself with ugly people, when you can spend time with beautiful ones all day?"

It was politically incorrect, but I could forgive him. He was a visual person; how things looked mattered to him more than anything else. That was his strength, and his weakness. Appearances sold things, but I hoped he knew there was more to me than that.

Scorpio

Friday night in the staffroom – enter Stephen.

"Hey," he said.

I was sitting at a computer, near the windows.

"What's with the vibe today?" I gave him a questioning look, peering over my glasses.

"What?"

"What sign are we now in – is it in transit?"

"What?"

"You know, what do they call it?"

He's not on the ball tonight, I thought. Unusual for him, he's so sharp.

"You mean the zodiac?"

"Yeah, right!"

"I think we're coming into Scorpio," I said.

"The sexiest sign of the zodiac!" (He's Gemini.)

"Yeah," I agreed. "They're interested in the body. They make good doctors, scientists, coroners and researchers. They tend to be mysterious, and secretive. Sometimes they are spies or detectives."

"Is that in your book?"

"It might be."

"How much more you gotta write?"

"Oh, it probably won't get published!"

"You know, I was stung by a scorpion once, in the desert," he said. "Man, it was a trip. Painful, but better than any heroin. My mind went. I was ecstatic."

"Was it erotic?"

"Yeah."

My father was a Scorpio, born on November the thirteenth. You know what, I'm thinking of you. Happy Birthday, Scorpio, whenever it is.

Out of the Darkness

This morning I was up early, with the sunrise. Old scavengers on bicycles were picking up cardboard, streetsellers in the sidestreets were cooking rice for the workers. Crew on the street corner were putting down paving; young girls in white blouses, black shorts and black jackets, worn from riding the subway, walked the plank, precarious on thin stilettos. A businessman clutching a man-bag dodged the traffic. I crossed in front of a waiting taxi. A white car hooted, and the driver sped off.

The earth was covered with a walkway, but a thin ribbon of newly laid sand was exposed. A red butterfly hovered over it. When its wings turned, I saw it was a Red Admiral. Past the park and the fountains, the drunkards, halfway to sober, stirring on park benches; past the DVD rooms and the guilty couples, sleepily emerging; past Lotte cinema and microphone girls selling cosmetics, dressed like cheerleaders. It floated along, tilting its wings leeward. My eyes followed it down and down and down, and then I let it go, with the thought of home, wherever that was.

Memories

It's Chuseok, when Koreans remember the dead. I'm thinking of the mountains, and the burial mounds on the lower slopes, where water drains. Like spirits, which evaporate – or do they? There'll always be flowers, blossom that blows. I catch a memory in fragrance: Peace, my father's favourite rose.

Twelve years ago, I was here with Sebastian, my teacher, lover, friend. Everyone said I was like Meg Ryan, and he, Brad Pitt. It was romantic. We came in monsoon season. And Sharon from Wales met us. I thought of Phil and his leylines, and Coller as well.

I remember my first aerial glimpse of this island, out of the plane window. I loved the mountains, the grey granite, the red earth in places, the dark pine forests. And the South Sea coast most of all; it reminds me of Wales, or Ireland.

At Chuseok, people buy flowers. My favourites are freesias. Sebastian bought me armfuls every week. I like the jewel-like colours, the heady perfume. Today, I thought of him in passing, and his late grandfather, who hoped we would marry.

My student friend, June, has emailed. She wants to meet me in a restaurant. But I'm self-contained. Almost every Korean family are leaving food on the graves to sustain the spirits of their ancestors. I'd rather think in the quiet; think about my father and grandmother and godmother, and my uncle, the professor, who died in the Strand. The Egyptians believe in an afterlife, and Mexicans, as well. Sometimes, I feel as if I'm not writing this. I know it sounds strange.

It's dark now. The night is black. I'm getting tired. I can

see couples, canoodling under the blue neon, students, casually dressed in jeans. There's noone in Korean costume, like in the old days. People break with tradition; times have changed.

Today, one of my students has told me of a painting: *Dream Journey to the Immortal Peach Orchard*, from the Chosun Dynasty. The colours remind me of old sepia photographs; beauty all the greater because it's faded.

It's inspired by a dream of what is lost, something desired that you want to touch. It whispers of unvoiced memories. It contains a wish. You want to reach for that which is attainable, but transient.

The painting was stolen. They say that someone in Japan possesses it. It's guarded and prized all the more because of loss. Some say the work of art shows the Diamond Mountains in North Korea. There's a replica in Seoul now, a reflection of the original, but not the same, not true. Is there such a thing as an original thought? Whose ideas breathe through me? Am I a thief? Do I dream my own dreams?

People live on through what they do, what they say. They remain and live on in the memories of those who know them, those who have watched them, heard them speak. But some are more silent than others in our consciousness; they skim a stone into a big sea. Minutes pass, no sound, a flutter, and dead.

The Korean painting resonates with stories from China, of the Jade Palace. It's in the Snowy Mountains. Hsi Wang Mu lives there. According to legend, every six thousand years there's a birthday celebration called The Feast of Peaches. The fruit ripens, magically, in time for that day. There's a banquet to celebrate on the Lake of Gems. The immortals attend. The peaches give humans immortality, once they have tasted them.

"The ripest fruit is on the highest branch."

I am the ordinary man; I strive, I reach. When I was young, my father lifted me. I want to sling a stone, a small rock into a pool, see it ripple. I want to shake a tree, create a small storm, and see the fruit tumble at my feet. I dare to eat a peach, remake Eden.

I'm thinking of my first love, my father. I was young, then, when he took me to the river. We went on mild days, with not much overhead sun.

"Be careful of your shadow," he used to tell me, "and keep very still and quiet."

Some people think fishing is boring, but whatever he loved, I loved; just to be near to him, that was all.

The box of fishing flies was like a rainbow, and as I fingered the feathers with the hooks, I wondered why so many – just one was all it took.

"The bait has to go with the seasons, to mimic nature, and then they don't know."

Hours passed when I was with him. He was clever, quiet and unassuming, deep like whirlpools. He taught me about nature, the kind of knowledge you don't find in textbooks. I never broke their necks though, although he showed me how. I hadn't the killer instinct.

"Everything dies!" he once said, as I cowered away, shocked at how brutal things were. But then, I was just a girl, and he always tried to protect me.

"He used to swim in the Teifi River," my grandmother said. "When he was young, his father used to scold him, beat him, see, cos he nearly drowned. Gethin should never have come over the Black Mountains."

I met my grandfather when I was nine. I'd seen a photo of him shot in profile, sitting on a prison wall. He was a conscientious objector in the war. He had a hooked nose, and he looked like a foreigner, with large piercing eyes, close set. My father had not spoken to him for about fifteen years, but Gethin wanted to see his grandchildren.

At any mention of his name, down came my grandmother's

fist on the oak farmhouse table. She vowed she would dance on his grave. He was a successful businessman, outwardly respectable. He worked for The Prudential as a manager and preached at the chapel. But he was a wife-beater, and my father had chosen to stick by her.

After the service, the Welsh side of the family gave me some chocolate. I had a bilious attack. It lasted for days. You see, to me, he'd shown nothing but kindness. I'd had holidays in Gloucester with him and Anne, who called him Humph. Once in the orchard, under the apple trees, she told me he could be tough. But she had no complaints. She was pretty, and voluptuous, and twice his size.

I can see my father now, at his father's funeral. One solitary tear rolled down his pinched face.

It was a secret that we went.

"On no account tell your grandmother," he insisted.

And I agreed it would be best. Nothing at that funeral prepared me for the one that would come next.

"At the going down of the sun and in the morning we will remember them."

My grandmother, my mother and I went to two funerals on the same day. I'd never expected such a spectacle. Such a lonely crowd of people who'd come to say goodbye. The noiseless black limousines glided past security, who gave understated, solemn nods, and the boys lined the drive, dressed in brown military uniforms, the gold buttons reflecting the sun, their black boots gleaming like mirrors. And they doffed their caps, and bowed their heads as we passed.

The grounds of the camp were a sea of flowers. We filed into church. As I watched the ghostly candles dance to the drifting music of the organ, men and women who had known him averted their eyes, their tears veiled, as the coffin passed behind the purple curtain.

I craned my neck up to the empty vaulted ceiling as we

prayed. We stood and sang 'Bread of Heaven'. I glimpsed my grandmother's face; she was silent, composed, and resigned. I thought I saw one of the soldiers crying, though. And my mother bowed her head until it was over.

There was a shiver in the air, but a cool sun came out as we gathered for the fly-past. And I heard the grey guns and cannons blast; they left a faint trace of gunpowder on the air. A young man, silhouetted above the crowd, played 'The Last Post', and the captain marched across, his kind face expressionless. The captain's daughter followed, and locked my hand with hers.

She was older. I saw Elvit and Nancy with the blonde hair, and there was Tom and Frank and Jim, the Scotsman. All my father's military friends spoke kind words. I couldn't number them.

He was born John. But when they talked of him, to some he was John, to others Jack. My mother called him Ronnie. "I'll miss Roy," my grandmother said, in a restrained voice. And I heard the lilt in her voice, like a final echo.

A smaller gathering came to the other church, opposite the library. All of my family were present, and Nada, and Val, and other friends who lived close. My eyes panned the churchyard as we stood at the grave. I was looking for a friend, who had arrived late. Then I saw the gaunt face. Ron Parkes and Jean and their only daughter were standing under a yew tree, in the shade. Our eyes met, and I ran to her. Her arms enclosed me.

When my godmother died, Colin and I went to the funeral. She'd been my closest aunt. I wore a black suit, a pencil skirt and a cream blouse. I had dusted the plain black trilby, reserved for such occasions. But Vanessa and her sister dressed informally. Peter and Brian, my Irish cousins were there, and Vincent, my Irish uncle.

"Where's Anne?" I asked.

Brian leant towards me and breathed quietly in my ear, "Daad must never know the details."

I whispered something to Peter, but he was furious.

"Daad must never know!" he hissed, glugging Irish whisky out of a bottle.

A minute later, Peter was amicable again. I changed the subject to veterinary surgery.

"They don't always paay t' bills!" he moaned, knocking back the alcohol.

Vincent, my uncle, a man of statesmanlike stature and a member of The Royal Society of Artists, was laughing with my mother now, as if they had not a care in the world.

"We're going to a party!" Deborah announced, spraying on her Prada lavishly.

Vanessa said she was going as well. I shot them a look of disapproval.

"It's what Mum would have wanted," she said. "We're celebrating her life!"

Privately, I thought they were selfish, and the professor looked bereft.

"I think I was wrong about you enjoying yourselves," I said to Vanessa, years later.

"Why?"

"Death shouldn't be a taboo subject and funerals so heavy," I answered, "but I was a bit of a stiff, then!"

Privately, I still believed my father was buried in the way he had lived, surrounded by those who loved him. He lived with honour, and deserved respect. It would have been difficult to be light-hearted, hypocritical, even. I don't think he would have wanted that.

"Doll was a fun-loving person," I said. "She loved children. She always bought me the most appropriate presents on birthdays and Christmases. She had a good sense of humour."

The grey eyes gazed back at me, and then the pause and tilt of the head. "We weren't close, I was closer to Dad. I'm proud of the books he wrote. People will never forget him."

"Do you remember the toga party?" I said. But she didn't.

I remembered George for his love of travel, his interest in archaeology and ancient civilisations, and churchyards.

"You may remember the name," I said, slowly, "we used to stay up late at Christmas to play a board game together, your dad and me, about travel to exotic places. You had to take ocean liners and planes, travel on trains all across the world!"

"He never played with me," Vanessa said. The ends of her lips seemed downturned.

I told her how I fell in love with you, and how you thought my question foolish: "Do you travel a lot?"

(The 'stupid question' was too subjective, and reminded you of a Canadian girl you once met.)

"He's so interesting, and modest too!"

She was smiling now, her face animated.

"Mum used to hang around Oxford for Dad," she revealed.

I imagined her, Doll; that was what they called her. It suited my aunt well. I imagined her in the city with the dreaming spires, prim as any debutante in a crisp cotton summer dress, sitting on the trim lawns. And the bespectacled professor, untidily wearing his clothes, beetling along those well-trodden paths. Then, at the sight of her lustrous, dark hair, he leapt like a star-struck teenager across the grass.

"He never lost his inner child," I told her.

"Yes, he liked cartoons," she said.

My grandmother was buried at Llanberis, at the foot of Mount Snowdon, in a churchyard on a hill. I remembered we had been to see it once; she had shown him where she wanted.

"I never thought I'd live to bury my own son," she sobbed.

Now, it was just six years later. As I heard the soft thud of earth as it fell on the coffin, it felt final. A lone figure, dressed in black, approached me.

"Do you believe in God," she said, "and the afterlife?"

I nodded. There was a presence.

"There are many spirits in the old house," she said, with a faraway look. "Some of them are nuns."

She was a spiritualist, a friend of my late grandmother. I didn't tell her about the song, the one my father had liked. He told me what he knew about love when we heard that song on the radio, on the way to piano. It made it easier, having this as a starting point. He sensed the end was close.

I've heard the song on the radio. It's sung by buskers in Reddington, in the subway. In Brighton, you hear it near the West Pier, and in Glasgow, near the hospital. I've heard the song on speakers in department stores and on a friend's stereo. Whenever I've felt like giving up, I've heard 'Killing Me Softly'; the choice of adverb always strikes me to the heart. The French call it 'the little death.' I think it's a good rehearsal.

A Young Love

It was night-time, downtown. I was wearing sunglasses, in the dark.

"You're a dead ringer for Sharon Stone!" someone exclaimed.

Lia and I slipped into a bar. The music was electronic. I ordered chicken salad with balsamic dressing. Cathay hadn't worked out. She'd got shortlisted.

"Keep trying, Lia!" I said.

"He's a junior doctor, but looks like a model."

The target was very attractive; I liked the way he laughed. He was dark, clean cut and laid back.

"Let him make the running," I said. "Learn from other people's mistakes!"

I advised her of a friend of mine, who'd frightened a man away.

"Make it a challenge – let him make the running, and think that he's won!"

"He may not do anything. Know what I mean?"

"Stop saying that!"

"Why?"

"It's kinda low class!"

"Is he looking now?" she whispered, shielding her face behind the cascade of flowing brunette hair.

"Just ignore him, he'll come over soon!"

I must confess to a touch of voyeuristic pleasure, when finally he spoke.

"So what do you think?"

"Too early to tell," I said.

"He asked for my phone number, when we were at the bar."

"Nice work!" I laughed. "Now you can reel him in, like a fish!"

"Maybe he's not so easy," she shrugged. "He's very popular."

"Keep trying, Lia," I said. "But not too hard. I want you to be expensive!"

What was in this for me is anybody's guess; maybe a modicum of excitement, vicarious pleasure, like watching a film of oneself undressing.

Photos

It was Gloucester, the time after Wales, somewhere in the Midlands – I forget now – and Reading, where I was born. I was tired from the comings and goings; they knew that I would never return.

"We need you," they say.

I'd tried again to stay, to go dutifully to work. But now, I was being loyal to myself.

"There are plenty of Morleys in the world," Julia said. Her partner had moved in her pub and taken over. The loss of her business and her reputation meant that she had a low opinion of malingerers and opportunists.

"No, he's professional!" I said.

"Write him a letter!" my Indian friend said. She offered to take some pictures. "He needs waking up!" (It was pleasurable, doing this for you. It made me feel closer. I wasn't the coy girl in a lingerie shop anymore.)

He was one of our regular customers. He always came in alone. He'd only let me serve him. Today, he'd have the French set, but he wanted to choose the colour that might enhance her skin the most. "What do you think?" he said. "Her skin's fair, like yours." He was holding the burgundy fabric to my face. Standing there, in the satin, I felt an erotic charge.

I remember Elaine; Elaine of the brunette coiffure and high heels. She saw me as I am: a sexual being, human.

"When you joked about your taste for men who are players, I think the joke was on me!" I said.

"No, I'm the one that falls for bad boys!" She complained

that her latest conquest was an alcoholic.

"Maybe you should change your script," I said.

She nodded.

"Be honest, Sue. Why don't you leave him?"

"I'm scared, yes, but there's also a kind of attraction. I like sportsmen who are imaginative and intelligent. They have high levels of testosterone, and that translates into good sex."

"The problem with that is that they are usually bad news. They're often violent or aggressive."

That Christmas, she bought me a claret-coloured nightdress.

"You're having an affair," he said, "or else, you've turned lesbian."

A vague notion of you, Morley, enters my thoughts. You are standing in a doorway, in a navy designer tracksuit. You say you're on your way to squash. Your face is bronzed. My eyes scan down to the perfect white plimsolls. I've turned up 'unannounced'. I'm dressed for the theatre.

I feel sorry for that reckless girl in love. The image was meant to be captured with you, the observer and photographer. Photographs – what stories do they tell? I saw a picture of her in a newspaper once, and wondered what this meant. She was comfortable in her own skin. Maybe it had taken years of inner torment, of outward protest. The feminine and the liberated – she was one of an elite club. I think she held a book in her hands, like a fig leaf. Through the years, she challenged patriarchy by transforming feminism. Some said she sold it down the river, but they were extremists, bra-burners. I wonder if you saw behind the gaucheness, the shyness. But now the photographs confirm my new found confidence. I visualise you as you are: a man.

Perhaps my lines remain half-read. Now the pictures hide at the back of a drawer, or behind some heavy tome on a bookshelf. The worst scenario: that you could rip them into shreds, or place them under a guillotine. Perhaps now they are just visible from a gaping hole in a black garbage bag. I hope this is not my fate. Photos contain your essence.

She says: "Whoever handles them can charm your soul."

My father took photos. My favourite one of myself? There are three. My mother had two of them. The first was taken in front of the mansion with the archway. I'm trying to catch water bubbles. Magical water bubbles. I'm trying to catch rainbows. My mother looks on, and she is happy. The second was at a smallholding, a white rendered cottage in the background. My hair is dishevelled, shoulder-length, in a white Alice band. I'm so in love with the guy behind the camera, I'm unconscious of myself. How funny I looked, with the gappy, lost-a-first-tooth smile and the second hand jumper, two sizes too big. I wonder what he said before the shutter clicked. The Italian took the third one. I'd put my hair up. He took it in soft focus. It shows a dreamer, someone lost.

"Have you any photos?" Julia, the pub landlady asked. Her worn face and a dowager's hump lent her an outward appearance beyond her years.

The Colour of a Shot-Silk Curtain

I am sitting at my desk in the teacher's room studying a timetable on the wall. I feel someone stare at the back of my head, so I turn round – it is Stephen.

"Hey," I say, "what was that you said about the sting of the scorpion? Tell me exactly what it felt like!"

His hand scrapes the cleft of his chin, thoughtfully. And then his eyes, dark hazel-green under the striplights, are a search beam penetrating the dark left hemisphere of his brain. I sit and wait. The low bass of the Canadian voice answers.

"I don't know your drug history," he says.

"I tried some grass once, at a party. I jumped into the Christmas tree, backwards. 'Cream' was playing, by Prince. I was in my thirties. Met this guy with dark hair, the one who offered me a second piece of hash cake. Sat opposite me on the floor, in a circle. Had a smoke. We left together in a taxi. We arrived at my flat. I left him standing in the rain on the pavement, and went in alone."

"So, you're not one of those guys who…?" He mimes rolling up his sleeve, and shooting up the vein.

"No," I say flatly. "I don't do drugs."

"You know, it was like heroin," he says. "People use heroin as a substitute for orgasm."

"Because it's better?" I can't imagine that.

"Sometimes it is," he replies.

"I guess it's like having a relationship with the drug," I say.

"Yeah, kinda."

"And the sting of the scorpion?"

"It was like a stone rolling on your back. You know the ones I mean?"

"You mean a kind of massager? Like the wooden ones in The Body Shop?"

"Yeah, kinda. But heavier, harder – more primitive."

"Like a phallus?"

His skin looks rosy now under the fading tan, just at the thought of it.

"Man, it just grew and grew. It took over, until my body was like a fish, flapping."

He makes a quivering movement with his left hand to illustrate. Then the familiar Canadian drawl drops until it is barely audible.

"You know, I thought I was gonna die – that was exciting. Like with heroin; man, it was a trip. You know, when you do heroin, that's how it feels. You think you're gonna die. So you watch it. That's scary. But then you go with it, let it flow, until it takes over your body."

We have both moved now, to the computers by the windows. On the side of a nearby building, you can see the plasma screen with the giant poker-flame, burning in 3D.

"Can I put this in my writing?" I ask. "You are anonymous!"

He bursts into laughter, rolls back in the swivel chair, and peddles it towards me.

"That's quaint!" he says. "It's kinda old-fashioned. You know, I'm flattered."

"I don't want you to sue me!" I reply, mock-seriously.

"I haven't sued anyone in my life!"

(I believe that. He's a retired CEO from a computer company; he's reaching retirement from teaching. He hasn't got anything to prove or an axe to grind.)

"You know, Suzy," he says, "it doesn't matter what you write, 'cos we're all actors!"

He's giving me the wide grin now, and his eyes are like mirrors – I can see my face in them.

"I've said before, you can write about me if you want." I grin sheepishly back. "How much more have you got to write?" he adds mischievously.

"I don't know. It gets bigger, out of control!"

We both get up, simultaneously (this little routine has played out once or twice before). As we approach the hat stand, I catch the faint aroma of Terre, by Hermes. My sense of smell has improved these days. We stroll out towards the elevators.

"You know, there's this book," he says, "by Becker."

"Someone told me about that before," I reply. "Becker was part of the Chicago School of sociologists."

This raises both eyebrows. He shuffles from his left foot onto the right, momentarily catching his peacock-like reflection in the long mirror near the elevators. When he moves back towards me, we are almost at a standstill. Then, more confidentially, almost shoulder to shoulder, as students start to flow in and crowd the reception.

"You know, they have to wait. They know that they gotta wait for him."

I understand the connotation, and nod.

"Waiting for the Man to Come."

As we enter the lift, the overpowering aroma of stewed cabbage and garlic enters my nostrils. A mosquito is circling the overhead fluorescent light. Stephen kills it in one fatal blow, with a rolled-up copy of the TEFL guide. We glide to the bottom of our descent, and the lift doors spring open. A rush of cool air chills our foreheads. Stephen's hair is blown about in the airstream. He nods and smiles. It is a soft, distant smile, as if he is thinking of someone.

Outside, in the plaza, a girl wearing stilettos is running full pelt to escape a telephone contract vendor. Stephen stands on the threshold a few seconds, then donning a Russian Cossack hat, he raises his collar up against the wind, and bids me farewell. He is heading for the subway.

I walk alone into the night, into the alternating darkness. I hear a rush of water, falling over an immense granite stone, enveloping the granite like quicksilver, like a web. A Korean girl, some distance away from me, is just perceptible in the light that dims before perfect darkness comes. She is standing by the fountain. Blue-black hair screens her face, her fox-like bone structure half concealed in the shadows. Her hard, delicate hands are manicured with claw-like, tapering nails, like icicles. She is holding a black metallic object, her head inclined, and is deep in conversation. She looks up, unaware of me. Occasionally, her feet tap a rhythm on the concrete. She is a lone figure in the darkness. She is waiting for the man.

Suddenly, a question rings in my head that seems to be answered by the sound of a horn. It is sonorous, like the haunting drone of a lighthouse on the edge of a white cliff, guiding the sailors home.

Initiations

Up above, a pale, cloudless sky greets me on waking. I gaze out, above the cobalt blue tin roof and beyond, into the russet leaves of the park. It is beautiful today. It reminds me of a trip to a temple, in the fall, twelve years ago.

The mountain god stands high on the hill. Worshippers are making requests of Buddha. They say: "He sometimes grants them, if you wait long enough."

As we approach the temple, I hear a musical sound. Everything is tranquil; a single wind chime, hanging on a wire, is dancing on a faint breeze. The suggestion of sound is ethereal; perfume in our thoughts.

Koreans say they climb mountains, but really they are on a human scale. There are girls climbing in stilettos, there are old men and women climbing as well. For the more ambitious, there are steeper paths, but we take the route of least resistance, with gentle, graduated steps. As I stand on the mountain, I wonder what it would be like to be a bird. Then, we descend. A hooded figure in a dark brown cowl and modest dress is approaching us. He bows his head, and offers us some chestnuts.

Further down we descend, past the hotel and the pensions. Then we follow the glistening river, wending its way to the foot of the lowest slope. People have built stores and houses. The mountains are a stronghold behind them; it is good feng shui, they say.

We enter the shade of a family-run grocer. The occupants stare at us. I think it is because it is rare to see Westerners.

The grocer's wife reads my hands. She starts to clap with excitement. People make a circle around us. All I understand is '*yeppeoyo*' –it means 'beautiful'. But I'm unsure of her meaning. Today, it means that I was young once.

Lovers show you different worlds. I remember the time on Exmoor. I was terrified of the unknown. We must have been walking for hours; we had a compass, but we were lost, and there was a storm.

My waterproof coat lets in rain; Colin's coat is new. We are caught up in marshland, striding from clod to clod, sinking slowly into the mud. It is like quicksand. Dark clouds descend.

"Which way back?"

"That way, I think."

"I think it's this way," I say, pointing my index finger in the opposite direction. But he is the man, so I follow him, and we retrace our steps.

We are back at the hunting lodge, with wisteria which cloaks the old brick walls, and the long, narrow entranceway with saddles and riding crops. It is warm and clammy. I am soaked to the skin. It is erotic.

In the morning, we sit at the polished mahogany table in the east-facing breakfast room, silently sipping Earl Grey tea from white bone china. "It's a fine morning," says Mr Hartley, an academic, lodged in the corner. The sun peeps through the dense clouds. He is reading an angling book. Colin answers him courteously.

My eyes are fixed on a painting on the whitewashed wall. It is a *trompe l'œil* of a garden, somewhere in the Mediterranean. It is exquisitely painted. There is an archway, and trees with citrus fruits. And I can feel the kiss of the sun on the marrow of my bones, hear the sea in the distance. I see a name that washes away as the tide sweeps in. All I need is heat.

The Window

It was a spring day when we went to the Forest of Dean. The sun was high in the sky; the wind played a rhythmic percussion against the leaves. Colin was creative in finding things to engage me. I think Henry Moore's sculptures inspired him.

We'd gone to the recluse's house one day. Colin lifted me high, high up, so I had a view over the stone wall, beyond the barred entry. I think he had a camera, like a true member of the paparazzi. The aesthetically pleasing bodies – some upright, gazing out into a distant ocean, some intimate and reclining – seemed to suggest people known to me, but they were shapes, nothing more.

And then I saw it, in the forest. A giant stained-glass window. The sun's rays burned through it, so we were walking through rays of fire streaming across the verdant pathway. It hung high above our heads, like a grand masterpiece in a gallery or church. It was suspended between the branches which held it, like two giant arms.

The walk was a nature trail, but it was also an open air gallery. There was a bird's nest: a kind of ball made from steel wire, and a sculpture named *Melissa's Swing*. And in the darkest part of all, deep in the shade of a canopy of trees where wild boar foraged, were little starlights which darted between the leaves, bright as those on Christmas trees; they looked like fireflies.

I wanted to go back again, to see the first object. The pattern was intricate, yet beautiful. The glass had many hues. It was pleasurable to stand still, admiring the colours. It was like a magnificent kaleidoscope; I wanted to spin on the grass anticlockwise, as if to turn back time itself, to the time in the woody clearing in the bluebell forest, or the time with Jan, when we were kids in Brookie Fields. We'd spin round and round in circles, so beginnings were endings and the sky spun with us as well. And then we'd tumble, giggling, out of breath, flat on our backs on the soft grass of our very small world. It continued to turn, taking us with it, carrying us like a wave.

And then the bird's nest. It was like a kind of cat's cradle, the kind we made in the playground, standing opposite each other, spinning fine gossamer threads between our tiny fingers. Or like the pictures I would later weave of animals and birds; metallic coloured threads spun round and round the pins on a black canvas background.

And then the swing, which reminded me of the one beneath the elm, and the one in a Welsh seaside town, near my grandmother's. Now I envisioned the rope on which Jan and I swung to the other side of the brook, with the frogspawn and the sticklebacks, and the overhanging pussy willows on the banks that we picked and put in cut-off Fairy liquid bottles that we painted. Then it became the rope, swinging in a loop in the playground, and the girls in short white socks dived in and out to the sound of a chant that went like this: "*Sitting in the kitchen, doin' a bit of knittin', In comes a burglar, and out goes she!*"

There were swings at a forbidden place: the fairground. Jan's parents took us secretly, so mine never found out. And I could have forbidden pop or candyfloss, which were bad for my teeth, and go on rides that were too dangerous. And gaze at the exotic gypsy fairground boys, with tanned pectorals and biceps, who winked at us and helped us into the chairs that swung until we were dizzy with excitement, fear or both. I liked the lad's dark hair that looked like Irish Frankie's.

And then the fireflies, like those on the riverbanks, like those I was going to see again; synapses that bridge the sparks in our brain, conducting them like lightning rods, so they emerge out of the darkness.

The Colour of Ice and Fire

A student of mine has given me a pair of gloves today. But they're not for cold weather.

We were in a cafe, having lunch. "This is for you," she said.

They were delicate, fingerless, in a red satin purse. Opera singers wear them. I tried them on; the lace fabric resembled a spider's web. Later, in the staffroom, I showed them to Stephen.

"Everything I write about is coming back to me, in gifts from students," I confided.

"Writing's like that," he said. "You're kinda sending something out, to a consciousness out there."

"To the universe?" I said, seeing stars.

"There are two kinds of writers," he continued, "the crystal and the flame. Italo Calvino is the former. Michael Ondaatje is the latter."

With that, the Canadian swept briskly out of the staffroom. His textbooks, which he held closely to his chest, had pages methodically marked with downturned corners. Stephen had the demeanour of an actor. His father had been a diplomat. For Stephen, impressions, and the management of them, were important.

Nonetheless, I trusted him for his candour, was grateful for the encouragement. But I found it funny he could mention these giants alongside my first-time work. Now I felt alive, if a little gullible. Fire and ice – he could be talking about us, skaters, weaving patterns into ice, tracing pictures skywards with the gestures of our arms.

"Are you from Nottingham?" the cab driver asked.

(He'd picked me up a few times on my trips around Birmingham, visiting the client base.)

"Why?" I said.

"You've got a voice just like Jayne Torvill."

He wasn't far off. I remember the turnstile walk across the fields on the way to pre-school in Southwell, and Mrs Merryweather. I remember the penny shop, where my mother bought me penny toys from China. I remember the Saracen's Head, with whitewashed walls and an arched entranceway with a cobbled path and a wheelbarrow spilling over with trailing ivy, geraniums and lobelia. This was the place Dad took me, where he drank Black & White whisky to heal his ailing heart. Years later, I visited the ice rink, where a policeman and an insurance clerk were made famous. It was called Silver Blades.

Do you remember Ravel's Boléro? Do I want to be the cape to your matador; you the tightrope that I walk to the cheers of an audience, the onlookers stirred into a frenzy? The moment I met you all eyes were on us, all the blossoms cast out into the cold. Were they for a wedding, or a funeral? These days, I think love shows itself like a first flower in springtime, the process mysterious, hidden. Love is quiet. You just know, over the years.

Love's first flower; my grandmother used to send us snow-drops every year. Victorians believed that flowers symbolised feelings, each having their own message. They used to arrive in a box lined with tissue paper, moist, like the first dew in the morning, soft tears, or when the frost had melted after the snow. Their meaning is hope. Gwladys called the flowers 'the first sign of spring'. She knew the months through signs of nature, not the calendar.

Masks

It is Halloween and the pyjama party. I meet Pearl downtown. There'll be just the four of us now. Stephen wishes he could come.

Pearl has parked her car round the corner. We catch sight of Peter, near the window of a cosy sushi restaurant.

He says, "These are my golden years."

We wave, and he waves back. And there's his Korean girlfriend with the pixie-cut and the small childlike face, leaning towards him at the table.

I sit in the saloon and wait. Pearl returns with Carmen Tara – she's back from the States. She's been doing a modelling job. She appears to be refreshed, if a little slender.

"I've booked a restaurant, are you okay?" Pearl asks.

"Perfect!" we say together.

Freddie Mercury is on the radio, 'Don't Stop Me Now', and we weave through the crowds downtown. Groups of men in their twenties and thirties in slick black suits are hanging on street corners and in the plaza entrances, watching all the girls. Some are in miniskirts, some in hot pants, the latest craze. Others wear tight dresses, all in black; one pretty girl, with one plainer. It might be the sixties here.

A group of Americans cheer at us. They shove through the revellers, into the road. We honk. One of them is dressed as a pumpkin. He's ugly and fat. He looks hilarious! And here comes Cinderella. And the Phantom of the Opera. A group of girls follow in Venetian masks. And there goes the Fairy, and the Snow Queen, with glitter in her hair.

The restaurant is tucked away in a smart shopping area. It's Italian, high class. An old friend is there. She's tinkering with the silver, turning it over on the white linen tablecloth. Then she glimpses us, standing at the entrance with bay leaf trees in ceramic pots. She stands up and claps. (Koreans do that when they're happy.)

We pour some wine. It's red, full-bodied, from South Africa. The waiter takes our order. And so there is beef with noodles, chicken rice, spaghetti, pizza, and the inevitable salad.

When we reach home, the blind dog has piddled on the floor.

"It's dementia," Pearl says. It's soon cleared up.

Pearl has prepared a banquet of cheeses and crackers, grapes, melons and nuts. There are rows and rows of bottles. We opt for the champagne first, and then the Bernini. It's light, fresh and sparkling, and tastes like pop. Two bottles remain unopened, and Carmen is struggling; Christine tries, but fails. Pearl is weak-wristed. I put the bottle between my knees, but no, it won't budge.(No one admits that it's a man's job.)

Our old friend hasn't seen the artwork, so we take the conducted tour. Carmen Tara admires the bed, and jumps on for a photo. Her hair is newly scrunched, her lips glossy. She strikes a pose; we all agree she looks hot. We all return to the table.

"I've been married twelve years," Christine says, "and there's no sex anymore!"

She tells us of the affair, which started two weeks ago.

"He's a foreigner," she says.

"Be careful!" I warn her.

When Carmen Tara goes to the bathroom, she says who it is. We both know him. She texts him, but he doesn't text back.

Carmen has gone to bed early, and our old friend has left; her husband's on a business trip to China the next morning. There's just Pearl and myself, looking through the glass.

"The school's over there," she says, "and there's the church."

The sides of the skyscrapers are red and yellow; so many lights it could be Manhattan. With a peck on the cheek she disappears with her dog. Below me is the Sincheon River, opaque as a black ribbon. In the distance, a backdrop of mountains arches into a still October sky that veils the stars. I wonder how the world is from your window, and where you are.

Landscapes are like people, unless you know them well. What part of me is hidden from you? What part do I choose to hide? What part is imperceptible because you fail to notice me? A woman is not unknowable like a dark passage on the last train through another country. Her character is knowable, like day or night. The light catches the portrait in different ways, that's all.

Her voice is like water: breathy, breathtaking, like the sea, coming to you seemingly from the distance. You catch the music, an echo in a shell; but you cannot capture her.

She comes in different colours like a waterfall, cascading over rocks and ferns into the valley. Or she is as serene as a still pool with waterlilies, where the carp lurk in the shadows, hidden from the sun. Her voice is all that she is, and more. The woman unbound, trembling, rustling, like a river, various in her possibilities.

Sometimes she is tranquil, sometimes mercurial, sometimes lulling you to sleep with a hush hush of slow-moving water, or else she carries you with her into the rapids and you're together in white water, swept into a river-sea and sea-river, and out to sea. And in the darkness, I hear you. It is nearly dawn.

I am awake now. An autumn sun's caressing my face. I can hear the dog's long claws on the heated vinyl. Carmen Tara appears in full makeup, Pearl's face glows with moisturiser – my skin is naked.

We have fruit and coffee for breakfast. Afterwards, I begin to clear the table.

"No, no! Don't worry!" Pearl insists. She has a cleaning lady who does everything. Suddenly, I think of Angela, and how she died.

She used to help me with my housework, when I worked for Michael. And then Doyle made fun of me, cruelly mocking what I'd said.

"When I asked her how Angela died," Doyle said sarcastically, "she told me everything about her!"

"She wasn't just another suicide to me!" I replied quietly, in an effort to state her case. I knew that domestic violence had taken its toll on her, and it had been final. In the end only a sadist could laugh at that.

Angela

"Clean the pine table with vinegar water," she used to tell me, "and use lemons for the fridge."

Newspapers were the best for mirrors. She always gave me cleaning tips.

"I used to clean for Lady Rothschild!" she said.

I found that funny, snobbish, even.

One day we visited the museum of the Rothschild family, just along the road from us. We were the only visitors. Inside, there was musty antique furniture and stuffed animals, their eyes lacklustre. I thought they were grotesque.

Angela talked me through the family tree with the crest, which was hanging on a blank wall. It was gloomy and dark in there, and claustrophobic, too.

Then I saw the glass cabinet of butterflies; it was Victorian. Specimens' wings were pinned back, some were cobalt blue. I remembered the time I used to fly along sand dunes at Beccles with a yellow net. I held one captive once, in an upturned jam jar, but then released it.

"It will die if you try to keep it."

Such was the flow of my thoughts, and I could see Angela in her house, standing by the patio doors or the garden path by the cabbages and the flowers, or digging potatoes, wielding the spade with the strength of any man, or feeding the hens that later she killed, plucked and gutted.

("Alice tastes nice," she'd said once, at the dinner table. I tasted the reflux of bile in my mouth, and nearly choked.)

The day he punched her she was standing at my doorway,

in the sun. I was wearing a shocking pink dress with a black turtle collar. When I held her, the blood ran onto my clothes. In my mind's eye, I saw JFK and Jackie O when he was shot. Blood had covered her, too. It's what binds us close, that, and feelings we call love.

I didn't care how it looked. A little milk, and you wouldn't know it was ever there. I took her in and held her in my arms, tucked her head into my chest until the crying stopped. But when I needed you, I couldn't show my vulnerability. I can see you now, standing in front of a chest of drawers in your bedroom, trying to conceal the evidence: your lover's jewellery. Traces of her were there, signs she was coming back. The timing was all wrong. I couldn't handle your rejection. I needed intimacy.

"I suppose you'll want to stay."

Angela? Of course he had to leave, after doing that. And then she felt it was something lacking in herself; a feeling of being stigmatised, a sentiment I shared, with the feeling of rejection; the lowered voices, the judgemental glances. Women loved to bite and scratch.

But then there was Terry. She used to stand in the front window, listening for the engine, perfect in her frills and scent. He was shorter than her, but he had a big heart and was a good listener. He didn't say much, but when he did it meant a lot. He came every Friday from Grimsby.

I remember how upset she was, standing in front of the cheval mirror, examining the scar just above her pubic hair. She shifted sideways – her stomach wasn't flat anymore.

"It's okay for you!" she said. "Yours is flat!"

"Not completely."

"Compared to mine it is. If I'd have known, I'd never have had it done!"

"You'll be able to do gentle exercises, when the scar's healed," I said.

But she was inconsolable. "What if it turns him off?"

"Then that means he doesn't love you. He's immature and superficial, if that's all he thinks about."

I didn't know how to soothe her, what to say to heal her wounds.

"Please come out with us," she said. He'd arrive at eight.

I told her I wasn't used to playing gooseberry, and that's how it started.

For Angela, turning her life around would be like learning to swim all over again.

"Imagine it, at my age!"

She didn't feel the need to explain. She was happy at first.

When I called I found the curtains were drawn. Colin was furious when I dragged her off the circular road late one evening after she'd been wandering around in the dark, drunk. Someone from the village committee asked me to collect her – she was lying in the middle of the road.

"Why can't they do something?" he snapped, stepping over her body in the hall.

She was my best friend. I had to rescue her. We pretended it never happened, danced around the subject. I created a distraction for her. We went to the university together; we met with one of the most erudite and respected professors there, and we chatted. On the steps of the Charles building, down Angela fell. When we went swimming, Angela stayed sober, whenever we went.

"Should I wear the navy dress with pink shoes, or the black with the kitten heels?"

She was holding the dresses against her frame in front of the hallway mirror.

"It depends on the effect you want to have on him," I laughed. "You look a bit of a vamp in the black. The navy is more subtle, but not as seductive. I've always favoured the little black dress."

She had dark brunette hair, cut like Louise Brooks, and hazel eyes. Her complexion was flawless, except for a mole, like a beauty spot on her long, slender neck, which sometimes sprouted hairs.

"I'll wear the black," she said. I noticed that her eyelashes were thick and clogged with cheap mascara. She took a sip of medicinal-tasting Campari on the rocks, with lemon, and we clinked our glasses together. It was a little early, but I have to confess I matched her drinking glass for glass back then. That is how I lost you: by creating the wrong impression, by saying things I never meant, by using alcohol to numb my shyness, by not staying when that was all I wanted, all I'd ever dreamt. On this day, however, I was as sober as any judge.

"I'm going to get him drunk," she said, "so he doesn't drive back to Grimsby!"

"Really? You're not serious!" I said.

She told me he was too introverted to make a pass – I could identify with that.

"He's almost a teetotaller," I said. "He has to be, because of the business."

"I'm going to put some brandy in the pudding, spike his drinks."

She was standing at the Aga, pouring wine into the gravy. It was half past seven.

"I'll leave straight after dinner," I said, guiltily.

She insisted that I stayed. She was putting her shoes in front of the armchair, where her bag was. They'd go out after dinner, she said.

At eight o'clock he arrived. Dinner was almost ready. I turned off the Aga. Then Angela appeared. The table was set in Royal Albert china, the roses orange and red on a white background and gold detail. Even now, it reminds me of her.

"Let's go for a drink," Terry suggested after the meal.

"Oowa!" Angela shrieked, as she leant on my steady arm to get into her shoes. She toppled over. She was out for the count again.

"Is she always like this?" Terry grimaced, his blue eyes widening in a mixture of disgust and astonishment.

"Sometimes she gets drunk, when she's depressed."

Part of me instantly regretted the admission; maybe I'd been disloyal to her, but he had to know for it to be fair.

I can see us now at the pool, at Stamford.

"I don't like going out of my depth."

She told me not to be a wimp. I started at the deep end, and swum a length.

"You're lucky, for a smoker," she said, "but a few more years, and you'll find it difficult to have a baby. You have to be able to breathe like this!"

She gave me a demonstration. There were children laughing at the poolside. Their shrieks of sheer joy bounced off the walls and were magnified by the water.

"Colin doesn't want any babies now," I said.

"What about you?"

They say: "Don't leave it too late!"

"You'd make a good mother."

I knew the kind of man I'd want them with. (These days, I'm a teacher. I give children back to their parents, and I'm a surrogate.)

I think Terry gave Angela a few chances. One time, I felt ashamed – I was a co-conspirator, peering behind the curtain as the fish van zigzagged, fading like a herringbone into the fog.

"I wonder if he got back safely."

"He always rings me, and he's a good driver."

He came to the village the following Friday, but never phoned, never called round. There was no fish left on the doorstep.

Alan penned her obituary, in the village newsletter.

"She was a vital woman," he wrote. "She was beginning to return to the Angela we all knew and loved, when suddenly she was taken away from us. She did a lot of good work for charity. We will always remember her."

I thumbed through the newsletter, over and over.

"Is that all?"

"She was good with the girls."

I thought of her daughters. Louise was the black sheep. She wore red and black at her mother's wedding. I think she went to the Shetlands, to start a new life as a crofter. Sarah, the elder one, who looked like her mother but was smaller in stature and quieter, lived in Belgium with her husband and baby daughter.

I'd tried to protect them.

"How's Mum?" they said, in long-distance phone calls. (I hadn't wanted them to worry.)

"If the bad outweighs the good, I'm going to kill myself."

I warned the village doctor about her depression.

"Those who talk about it never do it. It's just a cry for help!"

Nobody, not even I, had done enough to prevent it. I imagined her as she lay in the utility room, a character from Cluedo, dead.

Snow

Sometimes Angela and I used to walk by the river at Fotheringhay. In the spring, there were poppies, and we watched the painted boats and the travellers; people said some of them were gypsies. The boats were personalised, with distinctive, gaudy flowers, and castles in primary colours on a background of bottle green or black, like gypsy caravans in Wales or Ireland.

In the centre of our village was the cottage with the watermill and the caravan in the garden. The occupant made horseshoes. These days the system is mechanised. John's farm was all ramshackle, with his dogs at the gateway. Further on was the old church with the graveyard, and the bungalow where the clown's daughter lived. She always welcomed us; she told us stories of nights at the circus.

The next village was Kings Cliffe, where the hunt came in their colours. We always felt sorry for the foxes. Further on still was Blatherwycke, our favourite village. Over my house came the Canada geese, every year. They flew in formation, a black arrow in the gloaming; I can hear their mournful cries now, and it's not long before the snow.

"I miss Jock!" Stephen said. "I didn't think I would, but I do."

"Yes," I agreed, "he was entertaining."

"Where's he gone?"

"He's up at Gumi."

"Doing what?"

"He's an instructor now, for the military."

Then I saw him.

"Hey, Jock," I called. "How's it going?"

"I'm good," he said. "I still have my military bearing. When I see the other guys, I know I still have it!" I nodded, and wished him well. I doubted I'd see him again before Christmas, but he was there, last night, at the foreigner bar. He entered quietly, like a thief. People say at some point he used to be an Intelligence Officer. Someone had told him the gang would be there; I don't know exactly who.

There was Chris, his girlfriend from Puerto Rico, who teaches English and Spanish, the girls from Georgia, and me. Dean, my old director, was playing darts with his Korean girl, and the footie was on the giant plasma.

"Hi!" Jock said, sitting down casually at the long table. He was dressed in sports gear, and swung his kitbag from his shoulder onto a chair. It looked heavy.

"How are you guys?"

Everybody wanted to listen to him talk, but Elspeth was telling us about her last class. They'd been talking about riding. "One of my students said he'd ridden a cow!" she exclaimed.

The playboy of the eastern world grinned from ear to ear, his eyes twinkling with mischief. "Ah! I know how your mind works," he said, touching his knuckles with mine as a sign of conspiracy. He'd rumbled my train of thought – that was a surprise. Some say he nearly became an actor once. "You make everything naughty!" he laughed.

The gang went to a singing room afterwards. The sailor sang a T Rex song, Chris and his girl sang 'Come Together' – they used to be in a band. Jock sang 'Stray Cats' (it's his signature tune), and practised a song to impress his latest girlfriend. I sang a song by Karen Carpenter, then we sang a duet. "They're not brown," he said, looking a little deeper, and I told him my eyes were green.

Jock didn't sing at the wedding, after all. He'd shown me the Apache poem he was going to read a few days before he left. "What do you think?" he said. His eyes were downcast. Annika's voice was now a memory that penetrated his very being; it was the Siberian wind across the tundra, leaving traces of breath across the desolate landscape, stark in its isolation, yet somehow reachable, moveable, touchable.

"Do you think they'll understand that it's all about love?"

"How's the Russian?"

"When she discovered I was just an instructor on a teacher's salary, she didn't want to know. I want someone I can communicate with."

Soon there will be snow, I thought again.

"The Eskimos have many words for snow," you told us one day, "because it's important to them, for survival." (You gave us many more examples. In English, words for snow were limited; they had many more in their language.)

I think this was the moment, the beginning of a journey of discovery. There was something in your eyes, your smile, and your thoughts. Whatever it was sent me. I was looking into the distance, into the heart of a dark foreign country. Before I met you, I never wondered about the shape of love and its colours, and how it seemed to change as we wrote of it. But you sent me wandering. I wanted to know how many words it might take, to really know.

It is winter, and very cold. There are icicles against the glass, and frost. I am tracing a pattern, before it melts. Before it fades, and is lost for good, like memories.

I think I fell in love with you when it snowed. I could see your face in the distance, in the lecture theatre. Maybe there would be rows and rows of seats, empty. Maybe just you and me and the snow, like a giant blanket. How would it be to awaken to the sound of your breath, and to kiss you? To see the daylight cast colours in the snow, like rainbows, when you are flying high above the clouds?

You must have been standing there for seconds, maybe

minutes, watching me. Your gaze feels sexy. I can't remember if you spoke. I wondered what you were thinking. I was wearing the pullover from Cornwall, in shades of blue-green mohair. Maybe that is where we'll go, somewhere like Zennor or St Just. We'll take the coastal path further south – anywhere, alone. You and I, under the starry firmament, walking hand in hand. It is noiseless, save for the sound of the sea on the beach below and your breathing. In dreams, I know that's where we are.

I can't remember now the first time ever I saw snow. There is a chill wind from the sea when it snows in Wales. The landscape is forlorn without the sun, the light cold and the sea grey, but the nights sparkle with stars.

Colin and I went to Cornwall one winter. We stayed at a farmhouse, and ate with the family. Cats scavenged at the table, springing onto our laps, their otherworldly eyes focused on a morsel, while dogs slept, embers glowing across their sinuous backs. Nights were long. How weary we felt as we climbed the stairs, garlanded with helichrysum. We grew tired early, then.

"Where did you go on holiday?" Joe wanted to know.

I could hardly walk, my limbs had seized; it was a first for me.

"Cornwall," I said.

We'd been walking ten miles a day, I explained. Colin's hero was Chris Bonington. He didn't care much for people. That was the difference between us. It was lonely sometimes, but I was becoming fit; I'd found a new hobby.

Colin sometimes went on hikes alone, with a pickaxe, ropes, and climbing equipment.

"This weather's not for girls!" he'd say.

And I understood what he intended, though secretly I wondered about the danger, if I had the courage. That was the winter the snow came early.

Then there was snow in Brighton. I wore a duffle coat in the shade of green that suited you so well: dark green, dark as a deep forest at nightfall. Sebastian took a photo of me on the shingle, white with the first icing sugar dusting.

When they saw snow, they surprised me. I was in the gallery room. They were a young class. They weren't usually like this, I thought: restless, wriggling in their seats, unusually excited. I followed their eyes. Petals of snow were falling from the sky, like cherry blossoms. They were dancing in the parking lot, like dervishes. They transcended time in the ecstasy of the moment. It was a first for them, Shantibai said.

I want to see the Northern Lights, that's the best way I can describe it. From the first moment I saw you, the emotion was a colour, like an aura. I think the colour of being in love is intense blue, luminescent as the Northern Lights, or a rainbow, or the plumage of a kingfisher, or a dragonfly's wings.

I was thinking of you all through the festival. I went to Steepleford-on-Water, returning to my chalet house laden with flowers for garlands. I bought moss, eucalyptus leaves, a deep mustard-yellow flower, and dried blue stasis; they were woven onto oasis and wire.

Perhaps you were in America, or Canada or Cornwall, or somewhere on the southwest coast. I wondered if you were by the lake at Rutland Water, bird watching, or perhaps in the Emerald Isle, holed up in an isolated cottage, near Lough Neagh, close to the border. The holidays were long. With each thread, my love, I bound my soul to yours.

That Christmas was one to remember, always. The table was set in gold and blue and white, with Waterford Crystal. There were blue crackers with angels' wings and faces. Inside were charms; I'd made them. My mother and father-in-law came. Phoebe was silent and detached. My father-in-law was warm and affectionate, and complimented me. My brother's mood was light; he chatted pleasantly enough. My mother looked happy; her lover, Ron, dressed in black with a white silk tie like a gangster, was playing the harmonica and cracking jokes. We drank champagne, and afterwards had coffee, soothed by the mesmeric hiss and crackle of applewood logs. When it was dusk I ventured out, standing at the doorway. Pipistrelles were toing and froing above the barn next door. The bark of a fox broke the calm. And I was standing alone.

Art and Life

I'm teaching an artist; she's a fledgling dress designer. She wants to live in London. She's only twenty. I tell her of my cousin, Vanessa. Maybe she'll go to St Martin's, she says, and live in Kensington. We talk about *Vogue*, and what will be on the catwalks this season.

I confess I'm a shoe fetishist. (Something's lost in translation, but at least I make her laugh.)

She is asking me about art galleries, charity shops, the West End and Portobello Road Market. I tell her about my favourite haunts; The Barbican by night, Covent Garden by day, with jugglers, mime artists and entertainers, the Tarot shop, and the Royal Opera House. I tell of the vista from Hampstead Heath all over the capital; of Jack Straw's Castle, my favourite pub; of Ravi Shankar at the Albert Hall; of the changing of the guards; of boat trips in the summer, along the Thames. And finally, I describe a memorable, romantic scene penned by a musical genius in the sixties. It features Waterloo Bridge, and sunsets, where the Terrys and Julies of this world go courting, though now they're Harrys and Olivias.

There's news of the royal engagement.

"It's bound to influence the fashion world," I say.

"It's so romantic. English men are so gentle!"

"Britain's in the doldrums – it needs something like this to boost the economy!"

Last time I was in the capital, I was walking along Fulham Road. You strode along the outer edge of the sidewalk like a true gentleman. Only occasionally did you look back behind you as you changed direction. I recognised you. I took a last glance over my shoulder, but the sun shone, almost too dazzling. You had disappeared, into a doorway. You seemed to hesitate, though I couldn't be sure.

After the tutorial, a wave of nostalgia turned my thoughts to faraway places; blurry, beautiful images, like a view from a rainy window: miles away, yet sometimes close.

It was my father's birthday on Saturday; I took time out with a friend. We went shopping to Lotte Young Plaza, then boarded the metro.

In the chicken restaurant, jjimdak was on the menu: a mixture of chicken, carrots, potatoes and noodles in a spicy sauce. It's braised slowly, so you order before getting there. On arrival, you slip your shoes off, sit on floor-cushions at a low table, and enjoy side dishes while it's cooking in front of you. My favourite is dried seaweed. The Welsh enjoy it because it's good for one's health.

After the meal, we went to a singing room and sang 'Honey, Honey', 'That's What Friends are For', and a song by The Carpenters.

In the evening, we met up with Sarah's Korean friends in a soju tent. It's a kind of traditional Korean restaurant, with a bamboo curtain ceiling, billowing like sails. Old-fashioned paraffin heaters warm the eating area, which has an earth floor, with paving stones leading the way to long trestle tables. We had dishes of octopus, with noodles and squid, and drank local beer.

One of Sarah's friends is studying to be a laser eye surgeon. He's about thirty-five, funny, and chatty. He reads faces and palms.

"This is your time; you can be a soft touch. It's time to get opinionated – stand up for yourself!"

(I didn't tell him what I knew, or how old I was.)

We returned home at two and drank coffee. Then we went to bed Korean-style, on a padded blanket, on the heated floor.

As I closed my eyes, I saw my dad's face again: the wide grin that lit his honey-amber eyes, and the determined cleft chin. He was always the man, right to the end. I didn't say to Sarah, though.

When we got up at midday, I felt guilty.

"Is it to do with religion, being a Protestant?"

"Oh yeah, I guess," I said. "It's called the Protestant Work Ethic."

"An excuse to be a workaholic!" she said, peering into my features like a little whimsical elf.

I didn't take a shower. It looked too high-tech. I had a strip down wash, dressed, and then admitted my shortcomings.

"You should have said!" she laughed, as I sat on the floor, painting my toenails. She wanted to know what I thought of him. I voiced my approval. There were several to play off, before she had to make a choice.

"Wanna do some writing?"

"No, not really," I said.

She put on some love songs. 'Killing Me Softly' was amongst them; she hadn't known before.

"It's kinda like you were meant to hear it," she said, imaginatively.

It was Sunday when we went to the Plaza once more with Kevin, Sarah's 'special friend'. He took us to a cafe.

"Are you going to marry him, Sarah?" (I thought he was out of earshot. I think he heard, though.)

She wanted to go back to the store with the blue suede shoes.

"Get the black!" Kevin said. Sarah took a mirror from her bag and reapplied her lipstick nonchalantly. She was undecided.

Her short lace skirt lost an inch in length when she tried on the killer heels. He watched her as she pirouetted like a dancer, admiring the reflection of her pins in the mirror, which was placed on the floor.

I thought I saw his tongue touch his lips. Then she smiled

wistfully, her hand twirling her hair. Seconds later, she jumped into the air. And he paid, for the black ones.

She was airborne and I saw dancers. First I envisioned Louise Allen, my ballet-dancing friend. Then Lily, my friend's little girl at the refuge, in her pink satin, ribbons criss-crossing her ivory ankles. Then I saw skaters at the Roman Verulamium, on the lake in winter, and Silver Blades, where I gingerly tiptoed, holding hands with someone else.

Next I saw Kim Yuna, the Ice Fairy, and Jayne Torvill and her partner. Then the Harlem Globetrotters, at the height of their fame in Wembley, whistling a tune about Georgia as they dodged their opponents. Mohammed Ali came into my thoughts, a gentle giant the day I met him. And then my hero, Schumacher, with the lantern jaw. Behind the smile was a strategist. I saw him now, leaping jubilantly on the highest step of the podium. Then, the champagne cork popped. The foam at the neck exploded onto the skin of a frenzied crowd. I thought I heard an orchestra playing the anthem – they were singing in a foreign language. And the crowd cheered. Then I saw graduates, their tasselled mortar boards flying high, high in unison, like dark birds, to the click of cameras, the blink of flashbulbs. Last of all I saw The Lovers: you and me together, and a dance floor, a chessboard. Above us was a crystal chandelier, like a snow-covered flower, and a piano playing in the dark. The timing of our steps was perfect. We were sensational, and no one heard.

I remember Trevor, in a nightclub, in England's second city. I worked with him, and we were friends. He wore bow-ties and frilly shirts.

"Do you mind if I go out with him?"

"I'm not bothered, if he's gay," Bartholomew said.

Trevor and I met one evening; I can't remember the place, exactly. He had a membership card. He was the perfect gentleman.

"Do you play?"

"Fairly well, but not when there's an audience around."

We were talking through a business plan.

"We need a little music to relax you," he suggested, sweeping the dark, heavy fringe away from his light grey eyes. And then he glided over to where the piano man sat. I could just hear his voice. It was warm as velvet.

"Play 'Girl Talk'," he said to him.

The piano man's fingers touched the keys as he nodded. But he never spoke.

I think I asked to hear the melody again so I'd remember the words.

"Eee" said the big man, steepling his hands, his chin resting on the tips of his fingers, "Trevor Money's the best thing since sliced bread! I knew you'd be meckingsummatovim."

He was studying the business plan. "Did you knore'll be getting married?"

(Of course I knew, but the big man liked to think he was ahead, so I feigned surprise about the occasion.)

"I 'ave to say," he said, with a touch of amusement flickering momentarily across his mouth, "I'm surprised!" He waited for my reaction. I giggled. "Nowt as queer as folk!"

I could see it was back to business; he was hugging his jaw reflectively in his hands, his eyes moving with the movement of his thoughts. His elbow was firmly positioned on the leather inlay of his desk. He tapped his index finger on his right temple and then spoke as if he were thinking out loud.

"You knor," he said, in an animated manner, "he's got the Midas touch! I think I'll be promortin 'im, before too long." He was going to post him to Portsmouth as a manager – it was the talk of the office. (A call came through, which the big man asked his secretary to put on hold.)

"'E's got you to thank for that!" my boss added as an afterthought, renewing eye contact.

The Bullet

"I have a test," I told Vanessa, "to work out whether you can trust someone or not." (I was in a cynical mood that day.)

"So what is it?" she asked.

I told her of the time I nearly fell, when I was a toddler, over a cliff edge.

"You were skipping round the edge in a world of your own. Your father rescued you!"

I think my dad had gathered me up before anything like that could have happened. When I was nine, he hoisted me out of a river. He was always there for me, keeping me away from dangers, protecting me from difficulties. I was a cotton-wool kid.

"Imagine I am insured," I said to Vanessa. "So I'm worth more when I'm dead. Somebody has the opportunity to profit from my demise. Who could I trust to save me? Who would stand back, let me drown or fall? Or even worse, would anyone be evil enough to push me under, push me to my death? I know it's dark, but it puts things into perspective."

Vanessa tilted her head and paused. "It's like one of those dark films," she said, clicking her fingers to retrieve her memory. "What is it? *Double Indemnity*!"

"Life sometimes imitates art," I returned dramatically.

I told my cousin a moral tale to illustrate the importance of good parenting. I was out with Colin and his friends: Robert, the photographer, and his wife, a social worker. They lived in Appledown.

We went to a park with an artificial lake. Miriam and I were talking. Colin and Robert were discussing photography and news reports, and desktop publishing (it was a novelty then.)

Miriam let go of Emily's hand. She shot forward, like a bullet, towards the water.

"Look out!" I cried, breaking into a run.

Emily shrieked with delight at the reflections. Some older children, playing near the ice-cream van, were looking on. I plucked her from danger.

Miriam was unaffected. "I don't want her to know no fear," she said afterwards.

Emily had come so close, out of her depth. It was all to do with trust, taking care.

"I sometimes feel there's a dark side to parenting," I said.

Vanessa thought Larkin had got it right.

"Do you think we are born basically good, and if people become evil it's down to the caretakers?"

She was undecided. For her, it was down to nature or nurture. Silently, I felt grateful, not least for my father.

The Gatekeeper

Flashback: "You cut it fine; you nearly missed the exam!" I said.

"He was there for you, in the coffee shop!"

"Are you certain?" Sue replied, her eyes growing wider. She moved closer, her teeth biting into her parched bottom lip as she twisted a lock of her hair round her index finger.

"It was him," I said.

"What, Morley? He might have had another reason to…" (Hushed now.)

"Be there?"

"Yes."

"I doubt it!"

"He was concerned, and when you entered the exam room, he left!"

I had spotted Morley, ensconced in the corner of the coffee shop in an unobtrusive place, from where he glanced over *The Independent*, monitoring the exit route. Allies sat at nearby tables, their heads in a conspiratorial dance, their hands sifting through bids, details of charities and research sponsors. The room was full of the disturbing clatter of knives and china.

Morley was a quiet man; a loner and an expert at behind-the-scenes manoeuvres. He studied the politics. Soon his ambitious plans would take him away from here, and if there was a wake, perhaps for always.

In his mind's eye, he was revisiting the drive past, the day when Susan shimmied alongside his table, trailing Faith. She was oblivious to the scene in progress. Yes, it was Susan, with her teasing laugh and her wide luminous smile. This lasted only fleetingly, leaving the doctor breathless with excitement. Moments later, the curve and arch of Susan's back made a pretty silhouette in the sunlight. Draped casually over the steps was her elongated shadow – the mark of a fey being. She tugged languorously at a leather clip which held her ringlets in a French chignon, shook her head, and shook it once more for good measure. The mass of blonde curls gradually loosened and loosened some more. At the final tug, they dropped in an instant about her white porcelain face, décolletage and shoulders. It was an intimate act, committed in public. He was in control until that day, when I saw his eyes irrevocably fixed on her.

A perceptive onlooker today may have discerned from the pallor of his face the strain he was under. Morley's jet-black eyebrows lent intensity to his gaze. He looked up, almost by chance, as Susan was approaching the exam room. From a distance, Morley was scanning her newly diminished form: her slim waist, her boyish hips. Her skin was ashen. The unbridled blonde hair now seemed dark, dull and lacklustre. She was moving erratically, rummaging through her bag (containing a plethora of random items, no doubt: till receipts, lipsticks, lighters, tissues, a mirror, a taupe eye-shadow, discarded matches, her passport, numerous biros, a notebook, a card sent to her on Valentine's Day, and of course, the cigarettes – his particular *bête noir*). Morley glanced at his watch; it was just two minutes before the start. She was fashionably late.

Now he rose quickly from the chair, scooped up his papers, and headed for his office. He covered the ground rapidly. Occasionally, in the manner of a city-type, he looked back over his shoulder. He avoided the Pater-Noster, and chose instead the less favoured route: the steep spiral staircase. His steps echoed as he climbed two steps at a time. On the concrete landing, outside his room, was the department photograph.

He was studying the stranger who looked back at him with neatly trimmed dark hair and a compelling authoritative gaze, when the under-notes of a soft, familiar fragrance crept stealthily into the depths of his subconscious; he was led by the nose. Lodged discreetly in his pigeonhole, between bundles of research correspondence and departmental memos, was a book; an unexpected find.

He turned around – no one was nearby – and secreted the book under his jacket. In his office, he placed the book on his desk, and a steaming cup of hot chocolate on a glass coaster.

Morley's eyes were now focused on the book; the drawing on the glossy cover. It was a red rose. The inside pages were rough, cheap pulp. On the first page was a brief billet-doux, written in the rushed forward slant of the correspondent. Morley turned to the index, and to page fifty-seven. He was not a man who gave way easily to sentiment. He claimed he was a man who dealt with facts; he was a scientist.

Some time passed with Morley standing motionless. His white face a spectre at the window, he craned his neck, and focused unblinking eyes towards a flock that was gathering at ground level. The groups were emerging from nearby exam rooms, congregating on the steps. He was looking for someone. A child-woman came into the frame in a plume of smoke, her head tilted upward, one arm aloft. He tore himself away and paced the room. When he finished the dregs of his cold beverage, he conclusively squeezed the paper cup in his fist. He took aim. The crumpled missive landed with a satisfying clang in the metal waste bin.

Now he was at the phone, tapping his desk with his fingers. "Any moment now, any moment now." Donning his bifocal glasses, he began to write. Someone rapped at the door. Morley stood up with a start and placed the incomplete letter face down, under a desk pad of blotting paper. He peered through the spy hole, and let his colleague in. The exam paper was first class – no problems there. They had made a plan: the Sloane could secure a place on a postgraduate course. Somewhere on the border would be suitable; Gareth had contacts. (I observe that there seems to be an element of self-interest in this favour.) From soft-hearted Gareth: "Well, to be honest with you, Morley is a man with a particular blind spot where beauty is concerned."

Once all was decided, the Welshman left. Afterwards, Morley took a fractious call from his secretary. "She wants to see you urgently, about her term papers."

(Morley told Rita he'd agree to see her, but purely to discuss her work.)

Mid-afternoon, or thereabouts, a note, written in a fit of pique on a shred of paper, was now in Morley's grasp. This show of inattention to detail and sloppiness, the bluntness of the prose, would make it clear there could not be love – it was out of the equation. He wished that Susan would be more subtle and circumspect – he had a reputation to consider. Once finished, Morley placed the book into a drawer and slammed it shut. He tucked the key and an envelope into his inside pocket.

Outside, the sun momentarily broke through. The sharp white edge of a skyscraper was now receding into the distance, the glass taking on a surreal mirror-effect as the shards cut dagger-like into the puffy clouds. As Morley put one foot before the other, his mind was racing ahead. He could see the Lawn Tennis Club, immaculate girls with tanned legs in crisp, flawless white. One of them (who bore a passing resemblance to the infamous Athena poster), with a fit body, a pretty smile, and sunlit corkscrew hair returned the ball with a powerful backhand. "Deuce," the umpire shouted.

Further on he progressed, his eyes now fixed on the dust-track ahead of him. He crossed the park and the road that fringed the campus, heading for backstreets of Victorian terraces. He had reached the edge of the city boundaries. He crossed the bridge near the observation post, on the banks of a meandering waterway. Two women in saris, walking towards the riverbank, were carrying a decorative urn. At this time of year the river teemed with nesting birds of many species and their young.

A restless wind embraced the ashes, casting them downstream, flinging them like flower petals into the black eddies. It was a burial by water. The scene which unfolded might have taken place on the Ganges. She was young, Morley reflected, and everything would pass. She was fragile; clearly she was vulnerable. The juxtaposition of impulsiveness and recklessness with the intelligence of her character disturbed him He needed a woman who would stay, for always. It was twilight when the traveller returned, retracing his steps.

It was half past ten precisely. In the illuminated, contemporary living room of flat 22 (a tasteful, minimalist space, with low ceilings, leather sofas, mood lighting and blank walls, except for some black and white photos of basketball players, and a picture of a flamboyance of flamingos,) a seated figure was lodged at the window bay. The familiar shock of thick black hair was visible in profile. It was Doctor Raven. A flicker of a smile appeared across his lips; he was reaching for the happiness that eluded him. He was listening to 'Woodstock'.

The following evening, Morley was sighted along the avenue. He was on his habitual constitutional around the block. The night was warm; the grey tarmac glistened underfoot, as a soft rain pitter-pattered through the treetops. Su-Jung, a medical student, a file under her arm, met him on the threshold of some student buildings, at seven. They stamped their feet on the coir matting, placing their umbrellas in the ceramic stand. There Morley stood, his head tilted, as he spoke with the girl. Shortly afterwards, someone else joined them, a European girl I know. He was ever the gentleman. He let the second girl through under his arm, in the manner of an Irish dance. Morley met the upward flight of her questioning look with a calm smile. And she laughed.

Once indoors, Morley peeled off his outer clothing, which was like a second skin, slinging it casually over his shoulder. He and the girls approached a wider circle of his charges; postgraduates who nodded back with shy reverence. His voice had a rich, soothing quality; mesmerising yet quick. Sometimes his hypnotic voice was almost inaudible, except to the most attentive listener.

I joined Morley just as last orders were called. His black leather jacket now clothed a wooden chair in the corner. Three frothy-rimmed beer glasses stood abandoned on a table. He offered me a seat. There was enough time for one more round, which I ordered. It was here that we spent what remained of the evening.

He had the attitude of a chess player; whether the blankness of his expression was cultivated, at first, I could not tell. He wore his Ivy League credentials lightly; his manner was business-like, practical and logical. When he laughed, he threw his head back and snorted. His sudden smile, which illuminated his handsome sombre face, was also a rare privilege. When he was irritated, his agile wit, which he used like a weapon, blazed with sarcasm. Sometimes he was evasive; deliberately so, I think.

On this particular evening he was hard work. It was as if all the seasons known to man came to this landlocked town in one evening, and reflected in his countenance. When we emerged at eleven, or thereabouts, he muttered goodbye in the manner of an acquaintance. I'd known him nearly a year then. His lone withdrawing figure blended anonymously with the darkness, Dr Raven's quick, light steps becoming gradually distant, drowned out by the clicking staccato rush of trains, the steady drip of rainwater, and the clock of a nearby church as it heralded the hour.

Someone had been watching him – a man walking a black dog. As Morley entered the building, he hesitated. A motorbike was on the grassy verge. He observed that the biker, who was hunched over the handlebars, appeared to be reading a map via a torch-pen. Seconds later, the rider made off. Minutes later, the blinds twitched, and the lights in the flat went down. Hours later Morley turned, and turned again in his bed.

Throughout the long summer, serene moments of solitude were interspersed with anxiety over what, regrettably, he had allowed to happen. Soon Morley was leaving for a little island west of the mainland where he had family; he thought of this as home. He was needed at the house where someone lay dying. His bold spirit, his frontier-breaking research, would be welcome at the college. Of course, I kept his planned departure from her.

Susan was wandering through the park when the old professor approached her. He was a Lear-like figure, and a trusted friend. She was outwardly calm when she received the news. Then, quite alone, she raced home, retreating to her bed and the comfort of Green and Black's chocolate and her duvet. Morley would be back next summer, she hoped.

One afternoon, Morley took a detour along the backstreets near the rail tracks. A stone's throw from a Gentleman's Outfitters, Susan's flat was on the corner, quite close to a copper-domed Jewish mosque, and fifteen minutes from the campus. As Morley passed the windows with Nottingham lace curtains, his mood began to soften. There was no David Bowie, no Velvet Underground. No one was home. The end of the street met with Saxby Street, which took him out onto London Road and the station. Soon, the next train would depart for the capital. The familiar local game had been tantalising and distressing, yet engaging, Susan said. It was played at the exact distance from which imagination leaps and the heart aches.

At first, I hadn't intended to betray her. I saw myself as the go-between. I offered to sleep on her floor; besides, my marriage was also breaking up, and the commute was tedious. He may have chosen Susan, but here was my opportunity. I planned to do some excellent research, and persuaded Morley to sponsor me.

There were negatives on both sides. Morley, though athletic, attractive and erudite, was, in truth, a philistine. Susan, though averagely bright, was not academic. I fed Susan the wrong advice.

"Well now, I hear that you talked to your personal tutor!" (Morley's eyes blazed with resentment.)

They say: "Her car was parked outside his flat."

(Later on, when the scandal broke, Morley's reluctance to hear her out cast her as a victim.)

The Dean was sympathetic, but stern. "As you are aware, Dr Raven takes a sabbatical next term. In the meantime, you will recall he has requested that you don't sit at the front – it distracts him. Your papers will be marked by the internal moderator."

Susan's other former friends shunned her. I detected a similar cooling of relations between Morley, my supervisor at that time, and me. I was a constant reminder, I guess.

She said, tearfully, "He completely ignored me at the open seminar – too busy talking to that young blonde, Imogen. He was kneeling on the floor to get down to her level! Can you believe that?"

They say: "Imogen has good contacts in the charities sector."

Susan's very public affair with an artist only created more speculation. But there were no visible signs of jealousy on Morley's part.

Younger students, in their first year, were hopeful. A chance sighting of Morley and a blonde woman, who appeared to be Susan, as they took a sortie across the park and then by the river, had persuaded them the lovers could yet be an item. They looked so well together.

The Return

This morning, I was walking along an avenue of trees. The leaves were turning to copper and golden yellow, a blaze of fire in the cold white light of the approaching winter.

I had to smile: someone shook a tree, and down they fell. The Korean woman was harvesting chestnuts. Further on, a man came on a bicycle. He kicked the tree, and had the same result. The fruit comes back. It's because Koreans thank their ancestors for the harvest.

"I want to walk with you in the wilderness," Colin wrote. It sounded biblical and was the beginning of a love letter.

"I saw an eagle. It was soaring above the airwaves, high above the peaks. Then it descended talons first. When its eye looked into my soul, I thought it was you."

Eagles are powerful. Sometimes, it's true of you. Are you lonely? Do you wonder if people like you for just being yourself? Your power was intoxicating, but I loved you for your soul.

I want to walk with you in the wilderness, in cities and in villages. But soon they'll be waiting, and I'll be there for them.

Crescendo

Who would be there? What if no one came?

Such was the flow of my thoughts on the way to the concert.

Years before this was the scene: Suseong Lake, with paddle boats shaped like swans, and little cafes huddled round the water's edge. Further on, there were grand luxury hotels, the lights blazing orange against the backdrop of towering mountains, and the brooding sky, pregnant with rain.

I thank the driver; a swing of my legs, and I am out in the parking lot. People are huddled together, clutching umbrellas. There is rain dripping down the spokes; raindrops on flower petals. Solitary men in business suits gaze out towards the skyline. Nothing is still. It breathes and moves, like a body.

Rain sweats onto the perspiring tarmac. It is humid. A young girl emerges from a streetcar in a long black coat and an Indian pink dress, a butterfly clip in her hair. The engine turns and the wheels spin, a fan of water spray swishing from the wet rubber. She scuttles away, her collar up against the biting wind. Her thin white arm grips her satin scarf to her throat. I hear the fading staccato of her heels in the foyer.

Moon is there to meet me. He's a tall Korean guy, with the large straight teeth and the self-assured manner of a Canadian. His son comes to greet us. He's wearing a multi-coloured pom-pom hat, which glistens with water droplets. His face is bursting with overwhelming expectation, one finger on the plump bottom lip.

"Pleased to meet you!" he says in perfect English.

"Your English is very good."

Moon's wife looks proud. She is taller than I imagined.

I take off the wet rag of my coat. Moon is showing me the seating plan. The programme has artist's sketches of cherry blossom flowers, and marks the anniversary of Korea's independence.

An announcement is made. Men in dark suits carrying wind instruments – clarinets, trumpets and horns – stride across the platform. Max's neck and head and face is visible, floating above the wooden shelf that holds the scores of music. The golden metal of his clarinet and the dark rims of his glasses are illuminated.

Girl musicians are sitting side-on to the audience. Some hold basses taller than themselves. One of the girls sits centre stage. She's next to the conductor, an imposing man with quick, bird-like movements. It is the beginning of the overture.

How soft the lights are on the blue-black of the girls' glossy hair. Their lithesome bodies sway to the harmony of flutes, trilling warbling sounds. The prima donna makes an entrance; the fullness of her voice carries the audience on a wave, and then returns them. The bows on the violins are wings, the music a curve. It is Dvořák.

I am watching the man; every sinew, every ligament, every bone, every muscle is the melody.

"This was my last performance," the conductor tells me, signing the programme afterwards.

His signature is rhythmic, an ink-black arch above the flowers.

"Anywhere around here," I say, thanking Sam. He smiles, bids me "Goodnight" and drives off…

Soft spring-like rain was still falling, soft as fingers drumming upon drum skins, and onto the blue tin roof of the travel agent's. In the inky darkness, I could see the lights around The Bell. The tympani were fading, ever fading into the distance of my consciousness. My heart stirred with the swell of rainwater in the gulley. It wouldn't be long now, and I'd be home.

Magic in the World

Sundays in Korea are quieter than weekdays. It is midday, and I pass time lazily in a local Korean restaurant, just round the corner from the academy. It serves simple fare: bibimbap, a vegetable dish with boiled rice, raw onion and kimchi, a kind of pickled cabbage, and seaweed soup, which is good for the skin, they say.

Tendrils of sunlight are creeping through large windows onto white tablecloths. I notice a girl of around thirty with a bright face eating alone, and she beckons me to her table. She's delighted to have company, and is very talkative.

"I'm a foreigner as well!" she says.

(She teaches Chinese to adults and children at a language school, and has lived in Daegu for about a year.)

We discuss the Great Wall, and body-snatchers, and how winters in the north of China are very cold, as cold as in Russia. Then we talk about languages.

"What's the most famous folk tale in China?" I ask her, enthusiastically.

(Her nose wrinkles with amusement when I tell her I'm writing a story.)

"There are many stories," she says, "a lot of them come from other countries because of migrants."

I nod, encouraging her on.

"Do you know that most folk tales in China are about the sky?"

I seem to know, from before.

"My favourite one," she continues, "is the story of a man

called Hou Yi Sheri. He's not real; it's just a story."

She is sitting upright, far back in her chair. The wooden legs scrape the tiled floor as she moves back from the table. Her arm draws back, as if to hold a quiver, and in the other I can see a bow. She is the warrior, her eyes fixed on a distant quarry.

"What do you call this?"

She knows the word 'arrow' but not 'bow'. I say the word, and she repeats it.

"You mean he's an archer?"

"Yes, that's right!"

(I am stunned by the coincidence, but don't say about an unlikely Cupid.)

"In the beginning, there was no water, and no Earth. But there were ten suns. Hou Yi Sheri took his bow and arrow, and shot down nine suns, leaving one. And that's how the world began."

Today, again, there is snow. Snow is general, all over Downtown. People in winter coats, woollen gloves and headscarves are braving the elements. Flurries of snow blow across a frozen landscape. It could be Russia. Valentine's Day brings it back to me, as if you were with me here. All across the city, shops overflow with soft toys, chocolates, roses and valentine cards. Young women, dewy eyed, press their noses up to the windows. I want to be an Eskimo. My heart is light, soaring like a sea bird; bird, like an arrow, winging its way across the snow to the beat of your heart.

Something reminds me; it was in 1969.

The streets are deserted: not a streetcar, not even a taxi. There are footsteps in the snow, smaller than mine, and soft snowdrifts are against the poles with Korean flags. I am standing near the famous bell – the silence is eerie.

I imagine my father, his arms wrapped around me. It is warm, the windows and the garden with the elm behind us.

My father's voice is a soft, deep echo in the darkness.

"Look!" he said. "Don't miss this moment. It is the first time anything like this has ever happened!"

I could see his eyes shining in the half-light. There was love in them, I could be sure of that. He cleared his throat self-consciously as my mother opened the kitchen door.

"Do you want a coffee?" Mum said. "What's happening?"

She stood in the lounge, her apron on, her hands wet from the washing-up. My brother was tucked up safe in bed.

"They've landed on the moon!"

My mother jumped up and down like a girl. Six eyes watched the screen in amazement. The terrain looked wild and snow-like, like the tundra. It was magnificent, light years away. Yet someone had reached for it, a conqueror, with a light step, and courage.

The man on the moon danced like Nureyev in *Swan Lake*.

"He looks like a dancer, Daddy!"

"It's weightless on the moon."

"They look as if they're floating, in a swimming pool!"

"There's less gravity."

"Do you believe in extra-terrestrials, Daddy?"

I wondered if anyone lived there, and how far it was from heaven.

"What do you think?"

He wanted me to decide from the facts, but he knew there would be questions. He had a way of keeping me quiet.

"Look!" he said. "Pay attention!"

The human oracle had spoken.

I fell silent. It was rare to be close to Dad now, but my brother was asleep in his bed. I was sitting perfectly still, watching the large freckled hand on the end of the arm that carefully balanced the cup, while his other arm enclosed me.

The Return of Snow

I remember last year, at the foot of the mountain they call Apsan. Pearl and I and some students were at the arboretum, walking amongst magnolias and hibiscus flowers, symbols of North and South Korea. Then we strolled among bird of paradise flowers and into the herb garden, with the pungent aroma of rosemary and curry plants.

I stroked the circular granite stone, etched with oceans and continents, and I showed them my places: Wales and England. As I traced the outlines, the stone felt warm. It was sparkling like fire in the sun, and my heart yearned to be there.

How tranquil it was, wading ankle-deep in flowers, pink snow, cascading, tumbling down, tingeing the earthen pathways. And the sun was gentler there, the light dappled; light and shadow, soft as the colour of piebald horses. Soon we will be running, you and I, kissed by the sun, running through snow – pink snow – downy cherry blossom, heralding springtime.

It is night-time in Seoul. Delicate white tracery: blossoms in clusters, follow the flow of the Han River. And I am gazing over the water, down the line of the river, where it first began. The line of your torso is close against my back, your masculine hands around my waist. We're suspended above the water, silver girders shimmering and luminous wings stretching into an amethyst sky.

The trees are bedecked with snow, the air is perfumed; how sweet, how dark the sultry fragrance. Forever hypnotising, always haunting. I want to inhale the fragrance of your skin, drink from your open mouth.

The landscape is bathed in the honeyed light of morning. Sometimes the memory of winter comes again. And my days are coloured reveries of you, my nights sensuous.

The Epiphany

I am holding some photographs in my hands, mementos of my journey to where the cherry blossoms blow. I want to know how to draw 'pink snow' – write the words in Chinese or Hangul letters. The Eskimos must have a word for it; snow that burns with fire, snow that Magellan encountered in Tierra del Fuego.

A student of Chinese tells me of Gyeonggi-do and Anapje. Flowers grow near water, near ancient tombs. I ask her about names. She doesn't know 'pink snow' but she writes my names, the ones I've had since my birth. First my Christian name: 'Su' means 'water', she says. 'Zi' means 'natural area' or 'the way', or 'branch'. Then, she takes my surname, going by sound. 'Da' means 'big', and 'Va' means 'versus'. One syllable remains, which is untranslatable. Lines which lean together such as Y or V represent reciprocity and interdependence.

"The Chinese like to write in pictures," she tells me. "They saw things, objects around them, natural things, and then drew shapes and signs, symbols to resemble them."

We are standing by the lake at Gyeongi-do. Flowers hang heavy on dark cherry wood, a fragile, pale pink trellis reaching into the lightest blue.

At night-time, we are at Anapje. (Long, long ago, in the Silla Dynasty, emperors and concubines wiled away the hours there. It was a hiding place where no one else could go.) Each year in springtime, couples sleepily drift through the blossom woods, and in the evenings the flowers glow with light, pulsating their dark, musky fragrance; they flow through the river-sky like stars.

"How do I write 'pink snow'? I ask her. Diana is a migrant from China, and a teacher of languages.

First, she draws 'rice'. One of the letters is a star. She says it stands for 'white'. Then, she writes 'red'. She's putting the colours together. Then she sketches characters for 'snow'. Her picture is of snow: snow falling, like feather-down, gently, softly, onto a distant land. I see the outline is a window. And I visualise you standing there. You are sun-drenched. The snow sparkles with fire: the red heat of a faraway desert.

"So what of Egypt?" people ask – it's one of love's great stories. The Egyptians always knew (and Shakespeare, and his sister,) that destiny is in the stars. They knew that love lives on in memories, that we can weigh the heart.

Language makes us human; the heart knows. Memories abide in the body. Memories are treasures. They live on in the walls of our houses and in our objects. They are the sentiments which endure and sustain us in the infinite chambers of our hearts. Our hearts remember. Our hearts have this language. Our hearts sing.

I remember the Winter Palace Hotel, once a forgotten folly by the river. Today, it gazes across the Nile, an old ally amongst strangers. It all began with this grand river. Near its banks the landscape is fecund; beyond the waters the land suggests a beauty once lost, and is now desolate.

When first I journeyed to Egypt, I wondered what life I may have had. Across the river, I am the traveller woman. I am the bereft, my body bent double with grief, and my workdays stretching before me; days in which I endure, tilling soil and gathering crops, washing rags in the waters, feeding and guarding my children. And all of this in solitude. Life is hard.

Luxor is frenetic. I see street vendors and traders selling camels, street children in gangs begging for biros. Taxis, bicycles and carriages, pulled by muscle, jostle together in a cacophony of sound that assaults my eardrums. At night, a peace descends, and white felucca sails drift like clouds over a fabric of midnight blue.

I remember the moment I gave my mother the stone. I was an unworthy suitor. It had taken three hours of bartering in Cairo market. The sun wore me down a little. At intervals, the vendor brought me mint tea. The stone had warm gold flecks, like the dark, blue, starry sky. It had to be good enough.

The stall was past the one with woven carpets in a myriad of colours. The ones made in sweatshops by children of little more than six or seven. I'd fancied having one as a wall hanging, as a souvenir. It would be a talking point over dinner, Colin thought.

The rug factory was ramshackle with a bare floor of concrete. The rooms were cramped. I can't remember any windows. I must have been carrying water. We were guided through narrow rooms that reminded me of sheds where they keep battery hens. Then I saw the weaver's hands, how small they were, and we retreated.

One day, in the old Luxor hotel, I was taking a siesta. The bed was newly made in crisp white linen. Colin was sleeping. A green lizard was making slow progress, like a somnambulist, across the white expanse of the ceiling. I recalled how, as a child, I'd made a lizard captive in a fish tank, in the cool of the garage. Lizards blend into their surroundings; like chameleons they're unobtrusive, and good escapologists.

The Valley of the Kings has weird makeshift towns, with wirelesses and refrigerators outside squalid shacks where nomads with camels take shelter. "Are you going to go to the Gobi Desert one day?" one of my students asked. (I would if I were a journalist, with a guide and a TV crew. Or with someone I love. I think you know. Now I understand the only thing you need to fear is your shadow, and living people.)

So what of Egypt? There's so much to tell you. You lose yourself, without a mirror. I dream of an oasis, hear the sound of water. I see a mirage. Out on the horizon lies the Sphinx. The capricious wind plays far-off symphonies in the sand. A chimera gazes at the heavens. Here is the riddle, and here, the lesson. Who will be my teacher, show me who I am? Stars look down upon these ancient tombs and the sky boat. They alone will endure, as all we have is the dust.

The *Nile Princess* carries us to Aswan, where we disembark. A light aircraft lifts giddily off the strip of sand. Wings tilt and furl under the sun-clouds. We are heading back. We follow the river to Cairo, then the journey home at last. I give my mother the stone. It isn't much.

"It's very unusual," she says, peering into the depths of the stone with a clear eyeglass. "Is it lapis lazuli?"

"Yes," I reply. "People say it gives the wearer powers of prophecy and wisdom."

The jewel is an emblem, set in a thin gold band. When she wears it, I see the great cosmos in miniature.

A Beginning, a Song

I have a dream of sun, and rain; of ice, and fire, and snow.

It may be morning when you'll be there; ribbons of sunlight streaming through a window, or maybe in the play of candlelight, or the glow of a Tiffany lamp beside an unmade bed. And our eyes see the first snow begin to fall.

In the dusky blue of autumn I'll see your face, when fireworks are flying high, high above. The stars in the sky are notes to a musical score.*

I want to dance with you.

There are a thousand colours in your voice.

"Have your nights been beautiful?" you say.

*The Korean word for 'star', originating from Chinese, is 'sung'.

About the Author

Suzy's first published piece of writing was a poem called, 'Chess Board World', which appeared in a school magazine. Although she continued to write as a hobby, it was not until she went to university that her second chance came; she entered a poem called, 'Love in Autumn', in a national writing competition, and it was put into a poetry compilation by Forward Poetry. A second poem, 'Crystal', was also published at this time. Suzy was delighted, but the book had limited success. She had to bank the royalties cheque, (for just over one pound), she was so poor. She had wanted to frame it!

By the time Suzy was a postgraduate, she resolved it was time to write the story of her life in a fictional memoir. She was inspired by the work of Joyce and Woolf, and became interested in such themes as memory, identity, landscape, sexuality and the body.

After her MA course, Suzy had a dual career as a teacher and estate agent. During a spell teaching abroad, she put pen to paper and wrote her first draft, carrying the manuscript through customs at Seoul and Heathrow airports in her hand-luggage, such is the extent of her technophobia.

She says the act of writing and producing a novel is like giving birth, and regards her debut novel *Johari's Window* as her first baby. She intends to have more children!

If you enjoyed the book, please feel free to leave a review on Goodreads, review blogs or online retail sites. Thanks!

Lightning Source UK Ltd.
Milton Keynes UK
UKOW02f0743050914

238074UK00002B/29/P